The
Later Living
Guide

The
Later Living
Guide

*Plan today, own your tomorrow,
and age happy*

Teresa J. Payne

First edition published 2018 © Teresa J. Payne

Published by
www.elitepublishingacademy.com

Printed and bound in Great Britain by
www.elitepublishingacademy.com

A catalogue record for this book is available from The British
Library
ISBN 978-1-912713-00-4

Other books by Teresa J. Payne

The Good Divorce Guide: Facing reality when your world is upside down (co-authored with Vanessa Gardiner)

Hey We're Part of this Too!

To my wonderful parents.
Without your support none of this would have been possible.
Thank you!

Acknowledgements

Although there's just one name on the cover, it's certainly not solely my book. I wouldn't have been able to write it without the invaluable contributions (and moral support) of my expert contributors and everyone on the Private Client Team at Parfitt Cresswell.

I'd like to thank Lynne Gadsden of Grovewood Wealth Management Ltd for her generous and helpful information about planning our later life finances. Thanks to Debbie Harris, founder of Chosen With Care, for her wisdom and information about choosing a care home for yourself or your loved ones. And thank you to Felicity Bunt for sharing her stories and experiences, and for her enormously helpful practical information about downsizing and moving home. Finally, thank you to David Allan APFS and Stephen Wilson BA (Hows) DipPFS of 2h Wealthcare LLP for sharing their knowledge and expertise about pensions. You can find contact details at the back of this book in the *Further Information* section.

From my own team, I'd like to thank Sarah Reynolds for her guidance and information on making a will and explanation of the Court of Protection, Toby Fountaine for his valuable information and guidance about trusts, Alison Courtenay for her experience and information on putting a power of attorney in place, and Allison Tompkins for her contribution on probate.

And, of course, I'd like to thank Hilary Schlesinger for sharing her story. Hilary is an inspiration and example to us all.

Finally, I thank our wonderful clients who've allowed me to share their experiences with you. They have exciting retirements planned, and they've made sure they and their families will be well looked after. They hope their experiences will help you do the same.

Contents

Contents

Preface

Before my grandmother died aged 93, my mother became her full-time carer. Neither my mother nor I realised how difficult that would be, and I witnessed the devastating effect the role of carer had on my mother's health.

My grandmother was a tough, independent lady who managed very well on her own — until she had a fall aged 91. She spent several months in hospital before going home, where she needed 24-hour care.

We were fortunate because there was a Lasting Power of Attorney (LPA) in place, which meant the family could deal with my grandmother's finances — but the strain of being the main carer and organising my grandmother's limited paid-for care with social services resulted in my mother becoming ill.

We simply didn't realise how much stress is involved in being the main carer for somebody. With hindsight, if we'd had an opportunity to plan for a situation like this, we may have taken a different route.

My mother never considered arranging for my grandmother to go into a care home. She felt very strongly that it was the wrong thing to do, and guilt played a big part in that. But in making this decision, none of us considered the impact being a full-time carer may have.

Unfortunately, the entire decision-making process happened in a time of crisis. We hadn't thought it through because we had no time. After my grandmother's fall, we were firefighting — reacting to everything.

Providing 24-hour care in a home that wasn't suitable for an elderly person with very limited mobility and — in the end — a confused mind had a big impact on our family, and ultimately on my mother's health.

As I see my parents get older, I'm far more aware of the need to plan. I'm more aware of the need to fully understand the options available to all of us. If the time comes when they're no longer as independent and mobile as they are now, I want us to be prepared.

I've found it important to discuss all the options with them, so they can choose what they feel most comfortable with.

If they choose to stay in their own home with domiciliary care, for example, we'll need to consider whether their current home is suitable — and what to do if it's not.

But the most important thing is to have these conversations before the need arises so we can make fully informed decisions. The last thing we want to do is make major, life-changing decisions during times of crisis. It's difficult enough to make simple decisions at such times.

Seeing my family grow older has made me think about the specific challenges they face around mobility, housing, physical and mental health, and financial security. I realised there are two main issues facing those of us who are growing older or caring for those who are growing older.

When I started looking into these things, I had a real problem finding information to help families make decisions about what to do.

Information about the law, health, finances and investments, mobility and choosing housing, downsizing, and dealing with dementia is scattered. None of these things happen in isolation, and having to chase down lots of information makes it difficult to plan for the future.

The second main issue is us. People. We simply don't know enough about growing older, and as a society, we are unwilling to deal with our own changing circumstances. None of us want to face the fact we're getting older — and that causes untold and unnecessary stress in the later stages of life… just when we don't need it!

I wrote this book because I want to make sure as many people as possible have a comfortable and happy retirement without having to rely on help that just may not be available by the time we need it.

As a solicitor who owns a law firm, nearly a third of our work is with clients who are considering making a will or LPA, applying for deputyships and attorneys under LPAs, dealing with the death of a loved one, and applying for probate or letters of administration.

I also act for clients under a deputyship appointed by the Office of the Public Guardian (OPG), and as an attorney under an LPA where there's no family or friend able or willing to look after someone's estate while they're still alive.

During my career, I've realised that, sadly, most people are woefully unprepared for later life.

I work with many clients who are already in their later years and haven't planned what they want their life to look like. By the time they do think about what they want they've missed the opportunity to achieve it.

A good example of this is writing a will. Less than half the population makes a will. Most people don't realise how important it is and assume their loved ones will automatically receive their estate. That won't necessarily be the case, as you'll discover later in this book.

Many haven't considered their financial position, and simply don't have enough money to live on in later years.

Why is this the case? Why are we as a society so unprepared for ageing?

Because we don't like to think about death.

Getting older and less able comes under that category for many, which is why the most many people will do is pay into a pension in the hope they'll have enough money to live on.

But they don't think about how they want life to actually be. So let me ask you now: what do you want your life to look like as you get older?

Consider finances, health, housing and accommodation, your lifestyle, location, family, work, social life... do you want to live in town with all the entertainment and convenience and transport links?

Or will you want the peace and quiet of a country retreat?

Perhaps you'll want to move to a warm climate.

You might want to downsize, move in with family, or move into retirement accommodation.

Later living isn't just about the money.

It's about how you want to live your life.

The more we focus and plan for the future, the more likely it is we'll achieve the life we want.

It seems many of us plan when we're younger — to marry, or not. To rent, or buy. To have children, or not. Where to live, what to study, how to work...

But we get to a certain age, often when our children leave home, and start to drift. That's where our plans and blueprints end, and we're often just blown wherever the wind takes us.

We start to live on other people's agendas.

Is that what you really want?

These experiences have made me think about how I want my later years to be. I know what I don't want — I don't want a life that's out of my control. I don't want to lose my independence.

I want a life I enjoy. A life that's fulfilling, financially secure, comfortable, and fun. A life with meaning and purpose.

Of course, my later life blueprint may be very different to

yours, or anyone else's. But watching my family and clients grow older has made me realise that if we plan our later years in the same way we plan our earlier lives, we have far more chance of achieving it.

So why don't we do it?

I think we don't want to face getting older.

We have this misconception of being old as having one foot in the grave — but for most people, it doesn't have to be that way.

I wrote this book to show you not just how to plan and prepare for later life, but to show you how you can have a great later life.

Growing older and the leisure time that goes with it should be something to look forward to. With careful planning, later life can be wonderful.

I, for one, am looking forward to it! I'm hoping this book will help you do the same.

Teresa J Payne
Parfitt Cresswell
April 2018

Introduction

The Best Years of Your Life

Close your eyes for a moment and paint a picture in your mind: when would you like to retire? And how do you want your life to look when you do stop working? It may seem like retirement is a long way away for you, and perhaps it is.

Or perhaps you've already retired, but you haven't given much thought to your future.

Think about it now, just for a moment.

You'll have worked for probably more than 40 years by the time you retire.

Let's say you want to stop working at around 65 years of age. That gives you at least 15 years before you'll want to slow down. At least 15 years before you truly start to think of yourself as "getting old".

Do you want to just stop? Pinch the pennies, sit in and watch TV?

Or would you like to see the world? Indulge your hobbies? Perhaps help out your kids?

If you want to live a rich, fun life after you've retired, you must start thinking about it and planning now.

You could be a long time in that future... so what do you want to do with it?

My friend's parents recently spent six weeks on the trip of a lifetime with friends, touring Australia and New Zealand in a camper van.

Another friend is travelling to India with her mum, who's in her 70s.

And yet another lady I know of cared for her husband until he died, then — at the age of 78 — travelled to Argentina on her own, rented a house, and lived there for a time. Then she travelled to Europe.

Another "old" lady has been bush camping in Australia — in her late 70s.

It is possible you'll be retired for as long as you worked. It is also possible to have a fabulous retirement. Wouldn't you like it to be your next big adventure?

Whatever you'd like to do during your retirement and older years, planning is incredibly important. Even more important than at any other time, because your family and friends need to know what your wishes are. And, of course, you need to make sure you can pay for it all.

So let me ask you a question: How do you want your later years to be? Do you want to be in control of your future, or will you risk leaving it in the hands of others?

With this book, I want to raise awareness of how important it is to plan our later years.

I want to increase understanding of the stages of ageing.

And I want to show you that your later years can be the best years of your life.

Within this book, each chapter deals with a separate aspect of later living. You can read it from start to finish, or dip in and out depending on what you want to know. Throughout the book, you'll find signposts and recommendations for getting more information or accessing specialist advice. And there's plenty of room for you to make notes.

Whatever your next steps, whether for you or for your parents or loved ones, you'll be able to find out the most important information here:

- In Chapter 1, we put everything into perspective and look at the five stages of later living.
- Chapter 2 deals with later life finances: what you need to know, what your investment options are, and how to make sure you have enough money for the rest of your life.
- Chapter 3 explains your options when it comes to pensions.
- In Chapter 4, you'll find out how to plan for inheritance tax, so you don't give too much to the tax man.
- In Chapter 5, we ask the question: "Do I really need a will?" and go through the importance of making a will and how to avoid common pitfalls.
- In Chapter 6, we explain what trusts are, and when you might want to consider setting one up.
- Chapter 7 explains what you need to do when someone dies — all the practicalities of dealing with an estate are here.
- Chapter 8 explains why everyone should consider putting an LPA (Lasting Power of Attorney) in place.
- In Chapter 9, you'll find out everything you need to know about the Court of Protection.
- If you're thinking about downsizing, Chapter 10 will give you lots of practical advice on downsizing, decluttering, and moving home.
- In Chapter 11, we look at how to choose a care home, and how to make sure you avoid last-minute crisis decisions.
- What will you do when you retire? Chapter 12 will give you all sorts of ideas… including how to start your own business.

- Finally in Chapter 13 you'll discover the key to successful later living: Hilary's story is all about mindset, attitude to life, and how she stays young aged 88.
- Then at the end of the book you'll find a later life checklist, plenty of resources and signposts to more information and help, and information about where you can find trusted professionals to guide you.

By the time you've finished reading this book, you'll be better placed to make informed decisions about your later years. You'll also understand that living a full life is your choice.

Of course, you may be hit by the unexpected such as poor health or loss of a loved one, but if you have a blueprint in place and understand your options, it makes dealing with challenges far easier. So many of us leave important decisions until it's too late — by which time, our options are limited. With a little planning, though, a very different outcome could have been achieved.

This book is for those still working and thinking about their later living years.

It's for those who may be thinking about how best to care for their loved ones.

And it's for those who are already there. Those who want to understand how you can make the most of your later years and ensure you have all the legal, financial and practical things in hand.

Chapter 1

Later Living: Putting It Into Perspective

Planning for the future in later years is no different to at any other time in our lives — after all, we plan our education, our careers, having children, and where to live. We plan our holidays in more detail than we plan our later years!

The real issue seems to be the lack of awareness about our need to prepare — and our lack of willingness to take responsibility for ourselves.

We are relying far too heavily on the state to look after us, and that simply isn't going to be sustainable in the future.

According to research by Age UK (Health and Care of Older People in England 2017), the number of people aged 85+ in England increased by almost a third over the past decade — and will more than double over the next 20 years. By their late 80s, more than a third of people find it difficult to do five or more daily living tasks without help, and between 25-50% are frail and most likely to need health services and care support.

By 2020/21, public spending on social care would need to

increase by a minimum of £1.65 billion to nearly £10 billion to manage the impact of our ageing population... yet there has now been a £160 million cut in spending in real terms on older social care in the five years to 2015/16.

Age UK found there are nearly 1.2 million people aged 65+ who don't receive the help they need with essential daily living activities.

We need to stop burying our heads in the sand and change the way we all look at ageing and death.

I hope this book inspires you to take action and responsibility for what can be a very positive and engaging time in our lives.

I want to dispel the myth that getting old simply means sitting and waiting. After all, if you think about it, the older generation has more freedom than ever. You're often in a better financial position, with no mortgage and no kids to take care of. And you have more free time than ever before — decades, if you're lucky.

Even if accident or illness hits, it's much easier to deal with if we've planned how we'll deal with it — and if we understand how much we can still achieve in our lives.

So, what stops us from living life to the full and embracing this new stage in our life journey?

Well, I think there are a number of factors. Fear and lack of understanding of the ageing process is a big one. Most people associate old age with incapacity and loss of independence — but for most people, that doesn't have to be the case at all.

The media has a lot to answer for, too: whenever the media reports on life for the elderly it tends to focus on negative stories like:

1. The pension deficit issue. The Workplace Retirement Income Commission warned that millions of people face a "bleak old age" thanks to cracks in the private sector pension provision. But careful financial planning and help from a professional will enable you to live an old age that's anything but bleak.

2. Poor treatment of our elderly. The Health Service Ombudsman raised concerns that nearly a fifth of complaints received about the NHS related to care of the elderly. Planning for appropriate care and making sure you have funds available can mitigate this risk enormously.
3. Isolation and loneliness — which can be a problem if you don't know what your options are, and don't understand how great retirement accommodation can be.
4. The elderly are a burden and drain on our financial and care system, and funding cuts are making things worse. Carefully planning your finances for later years means you won't have to rely on our care system, and funding cuts will make very little difference to your standard of living.

Negative stories like these are certainly enough to put anyone off thinking about their later years. But when we think about retirement and later living, the age we're really referring to is when you stop working. So what sort of life do you want to live then?

The true elderly care side of later living comes much later for many of us. There's a whole new life out there waiting to be lived if we only take the time and plan the life we want when we reach that stage.

But we do need to plan and ensure we make the most of the financial and social options available to us. We need to think about this as early as possible and take action now, so we're able to make the right decisions when the time comes.

Before we dive into the financial, social, legal, and other aspects of later living it's helpful to understand the different stages of ageing. It's also helpful to remember life is a journey and our later years are just another part of that journey.

Just as youth is broken down into "baby", "child", and "teenager", later living has its own stages, too.

Dr Mark Frankel developed the stages of ageing and I've

used his model here. Some of us will go through all the stages and some will skip one or more of them. It's worth noting many people will stay at stage one for many years.

When we understand the stages of ageing we may go through it becomes much easier to plan what your potential needs are.

Later Living Stage 1: Self-sufficiency

You are independent and self-reliant. You may be healthy or able to manage chronic health problems and disabilities on your own with little need for help. This stage continues for many people for many years.

Stage 1 is a good time to consider what legal documents you need to make sure life runs smoothly should a crisis occur. Check your will is up to date and that you've taken estate planning advice to ensure you pay as little inheritance tax as possible on your death.

Make a Lasting Power of Attorney to ensure your finances are looked after in case you're unable to deal with them through incapacity. Assess your home and community and question whether this will be suitable should your circumstances change during the years ahead.

Later Living Stage 2: Interdependence

At the second stage of later living, you'll rely more on others such as your partner, family, and friends for help. You may wish to consider options such as meal plans, cleaning and laundry services.

Later Living Stage 3: Dependency

Dependency often involves personal care assistance and help with daily living activities like bathing, cooking, and shopping. You may suffer from multiple chronic conditions and pain.

Later Living Stage 4: Crisis management

Informal care given by family and friends is now insufficient. Professional care may be an option but may be expensive —

and in some cases too expensive, unless you've planned for this and factored it into your later living costs.

Family and friends stay in crisis management unless they and you can find a solution to professional care. This is a stressful and challenging time for everyone and you remain dependent on others for your care.

Later Living Stage 5: End of Life

The final phase occurs when you need to move to a nursing home or hospice care. You'll need end of life care and your family will often have to make painful end of life decisions on your behalf.

Summary

It's helpful to use these five stages of later living as a framework for understanding your potential needs when planning for your later living years.

Careful planning means:

- You'll be better prepared financially — not just to take care of your basic needs, but to have fun!
- You'll retain control and keep your independence for as long as possible.
- You'll be able to communicate your health care needs and decisions clearly and document them in an LPA.
- You'll have a healthier and less stressful life.
- You'll understand the options you have available to you should you need long-term care.
- You'll have all the legal documents, like an LPA and your will, in place so you can be sure your wishes are carried out in the event of incapacity or death.

Now we've set the scene and you've got a better idea of what lies ahead, let's start planning.

Money isn't everything. But when you have enough of it, it means you don't have to worry about your future. And if you have more than enough, you'll have many more options open to you and many more opportunities to enjoy your retirement.

So we'll start with money. In Chapter 2, we'll look at your later living finances and help you plan for the future.

Your Notes

Chapter 2

Finances and Later Living

How are your finances looking? Will you have enough money to last you through your retirement — and beyond?

Most people are terrified they won't be able to afford good care but if you own your home, and plan properly, and pay for your own care you should be able to afford it. Not only that, you'll be able to have a wonderful retirement and old age.

It all comes down to planning.

Planning for old age is extremely important, even more important than at any other time because our income generally isn't going to go up. So we have to make what we do have last.

Which means we have to pull our heads out of the sand and look ageing full in the face.

At the time of writing this book, there are more than 12 million people aged 65 or over living in the UK — and more than 1.6 million of them are aged 85 or over. That's 2.3% of the population.

By 2086 the number of people aged 85 or over living in the

UK is expected to increase to approximately 7.4 million — which is 8.7% of the population.

And 15% of today's population aged 85+ are currently living in a care setting.

All these statistics are by way of saying: our population is getting older. Those numbers are going to go up.

Ageing happens to us all — hopefully!

Then, eventually, we'll all die. It's a natural part of life.

And yet we don't talk about any of this. We don't plan for old age and the end of life. We don't even think about it.

It's the elephant in the room, and the elephant is getting bigger and angrier.

The plain fact is, things are changing. Current generations just don't have the pensions previous generations had. Final salary schemes are dying out, property investments are rising, and although we should get a state pension it may well be there isn't enough money for us all.

Simply put: there will be much less money available to take care of the future ageing population, and there will be many more of us who need that money. We are all living longer and ultimately it's up to each individual to make sure we're going to be okay. We can't — and shouldn't — rely on outside institutions to take care of us.

Fewer than three in ten people at retirement age have any plans in place to fund their retirement and long-term care, according to the Financial Capability Strategy for the UK.

It's not all doom and gloom, though. We can each make sure we have enough money to see us through the rest of our lives, and not just enough to survive on, either — enough to have a wonderful retirement and leave some money to our children.

It just takes some careful planning, which is what this chapter is all about.

First, though, I'm hoping this book will encourage all of us to be more open about later living and the end of life. Thinking about it and talking about it is the first step. Once we're talking, we can start planning and putting practical measures in place to make things as easy as possible.

So start small. Start with your practical finances as they stand at the moment.

List all your bank accounts, pensions, investments, and any other cash or assets you might have hidden away. Get it all out in the open.

Then make sure you'll have access to it if anything should happen to your partner.

For example, if all your money is in your spouse's name, and your spouse dies first, you won't have access to any cash. It will be stuck in probate. So make sure you have a joint account, or split your money between both partners.

Things are changing, but for the older generation at the moment more men than women tend to have pensions. If your partner has a pension, but you don't — will that pension pass onto you?

What will happen to your wealth when one partner dies? Then, when you're both gone, where does your wealth go then? How much inheritance tax will your beneficiaries have to pay?

The bottom line is, you don't know how long you're going to be around and you don't know how long you're going to be in care, so you need to make sure your money lasts at least as long as you do.

The good news is, though, you don't have to stumble along alone. There are specialists out there who can help you.

What's The Worst That Can Happen?

I'd like to share a scenario that's far too common.

It happens because we don't plan and because we simply don't know enough about what we need to do to secure our future.

I'd like to talk about Rose. Rose is in her late 70s and has mild dementia. She's still quite young, so may live for another 20 years. She wants to live in a nice care home — who doesn't?

— and her family have found a lovely one.

Rose moved in, and was very happy there for six years... until her money ran out.

The family hadn't planned and hadn't taken any advice, and hadn't realised Rose simply couldn't afford her care home.

Care homes often only ask for two years' proof of income, and Rose's £15,000 per year plus the money from selling her house wasn't enough. The care home fees were £75,000 a year. For Rose to stay, she would have to find another £60,000 a year and it just wasn't possible.

Rose had to move from her lovely care home into a much cheaper one — and her health deteriorated fast. Not because the cheaper home was awful, but because the trauma of moving home in her 80s was too much for her.

The sad part is, if she and her family had taken specialist later living financial advice and planned properly, this might never have happened.

Rose's story is fictional, but it's based on reality. This situation happens far too often and it's easily avoidable. It's common for people to move into care homes they can easily afford for a couple of years, only to find the money runs out and they have to move on.

Care homes hate asking people to leave — most of them are run by incredibly caring people. But care homes are not charities and they cannot afford to subsidise people.

Nor can the government.

You might be thinking the UK has a safety net and Local Authority funding will step in to help, but that's the last thing you want to have to deal with. Local Authorities are extremely difficult to deal with, and they simply don't have enough money to help everyone. And a Local Authority care home is almost certainly not the type of place you'd choose for yourself.

Please plan early and plan well, and make sure you can afford to support yourself.

Step one is discovering what your current financial situation is and checking what benefits you're entitled to.

Step two is getting professional advice from a later living specialist.

Planning For Care

You want to avoid the worst-case scenario, so start planning as soon as possible — even as early as in your 60s during your early retirement. Almost everyone leaves it too late. Talk to your family. Talk to experts. And start thinking about where you'd like to go, what you want to happen in your later years, and whether you'll be able to afford what you want.

The sooner you start thinking and planning, the more likely you'll get the outcome you want.

It's very common for people to make the big mistake of giving all their money away or even giving away their home, so it's not taken into account when calculating benefits for care home fees.

If you intentionally reduce your assets — money, property, or income — so they won't be included in any financial assessment for care home fees, it's called "deprivation of assets". If your local council decides you've deliberately reduced your assets to avoid paying care home fees, they may still calculate your fees as if you still owned the assets.

In this case, you'd lose your home and your money, but still have to pay the full care home fees — with no guarantee you'd be able to recover your gifts from whomever you gave them to.

But it's totally unnecessary! You do have to pay for your own care, but you don't have to spend all your money on it if you plan carefully.

And as for local authority care, it's a safety net for those who have no money or assets at all. You don't want to end up in local authority care because it's not the care you would choose for yourself. It's chosen by someone else, and it's a last resort.

By getting professional specialist advice and planning carefully you should be able to ring-fence the money that goes into your care and use the rest in any way you please.

One of our clients was a man in his early 80s with mild dementia. He sold his house and now has around £500,000 in assets. He's living in a care home and having a fantastic time.

If he does nothing with his money, he'll run out when he's 90... but what if he lives longer? As you now know, running out of cash is the worst-case scenario. His pension will only increase slightly with inflation. But the care home fees will carry on and will, more than likely, increase at a rate generally higher than inflation.

So how do we ensure our gentleman has enough money to pay for his care forever — and enough to leave some for his family?

By buying a care fees annuity for £250,000. This specialist annuity will pay out an amount to the care home each year for the rest of his life, and will even keep up with inflation. By consulting an expert, he and his family worked out his finances so his income will carry on forever — even if he lives to be 103.

£250,000 sounds like an awful lot of money, and it is. But because he used it to buy an annuity, the care home will receive the amount he covered for the rest of his life. And he still has more than £200,000 left over to enjoy and to pass onto his family.

His family no longer has to worry about him. He knows he's safe and sound and won't have to move from his lovely care home.

If he dies early, the annuity may have cost more than it paid for in care — but if he lives for a long time, it's fantastic value.

And even if he doesn't live as long as he might hope, the peace of mind that comes from knowing you'll never have to move from your care home and you'll never run out of money is priceless.

Annuities aren't your only option so, as always, my best advice is to talk to a specialist later living financial advisor to find out what's best for you.

And after your care home comes the final big event of your life...

The High Cost of Dying

Although it's the most natural thing in the world, we're not very good at talking about it. And that's a problem because dying can be an expensive business.

Death can cause financial as well as emotional grief — which is why planning for the last big event of your life isn't morbid, it's vital. Your family will be dealing with losing a loved one, so if you can make the practicalities as simple as possible for them, they'll have a much easier time.

At the time of writing this book, the average cost of a funeral in the UK is £4,257 for a traditional burial or £3,311 for a cremation. By 2021, the cost is likely to rise to £4,779.

And that's just for the basics: funeral directors' fees, cremation or burial, gravesite, transport, venue, ceremony, and local authority fees.

You'll also need to factor in flowers, doctors' fees, an obituary in the newspaper, orders of service, and catering. And if you want a memorial of some kind, that will cost extra too.

If you and your family want a bit of a do, it'll cost much more. It's not unknown for fancy funerals to cost as much as a wedding.

Plus, if you're likely to be living abroad, you'll have to consider the cost of repatriation, which can be expensive.

It's a good idea to put money aside early on so your family doesn't have to worry about funeral costs, and you don't have to worry about them.

A good way to do this is with a funeral plan. Age UK has some great information about their approved plans. A funeral plan will cover most of the costs of your funeral in advance and will provide support for you and your family. With a good plan, you'll get guidance from a trusted funeral director and your family will get access to bereavement counselling if they need it.

If you do decide to open a funeral plan, make sure it's independent so you can choose any funeral director you like.

If you decide not to open a funeral plan, the costs for your funeral will come out of your estate — which means your beneficiaries of your will receive less.

If your estate won't cover the costs and your family can't afford your funeral, the government provides a Social Fund to help loved ones cover the costs of a funeral. It will only cover a portion of the costs, and you or the deceased must have been claiming benefits in order to be eligible. You'll also need to prove there's no one else related to the deceased who could reasonably be expected to pay the funeral costs. You have to fill in a 23-page form to apply and you may not receive the funds until after the funeral because it can take a couple of weeks to process applications.

If you genuinely can't pay anything at all, local authorities have a legal duty to make arrangements and will provide a public health funeral. This often happens for homeless people with no family, and are the last resort. They weren't designed for people who can't afford to pay for a funeral, but they're sometimes used for this reason when people genuinely have no other option.

You don't want you or your family to be in this position, so if you can make arrangements in advance, it's a good idea to do so. A specialist financial advisor will be able to help you make a plan.

Take Care of Your Pension

Of course, hopefully you're going to be around for a good long time before funerals start looming. So, in the meantime, let's make sure you have enough money to enjoy yourself!

You want an income in your retirement, to make sure you're comfortable and taken care of, but also to make sure you can enjoy life.

People are living longer than ever before, which is great news — but it means when you retire, your money has to last longer. You can spend between 30 and 40 years building your pension fund to support your retirement and it will probably be your biggest asset when you do retire. It has to last you for the rest of your life — which could be as long as another 40 years if you're lucky. Choosing how to take funds from your pension could be the biggest financial decision you'll ever make.

It's a very complicated area and you should definitely get advice.

Build your pension planning into your general later life financial planning. Chapter 3 explains your pension options in detail including, how to take care of your pension, how to avoid giving all your wealth to the taxman, and how to manage your finances in this new phase of later life.

Managing Your Finances

When it comes to later life finances, remember: keep it simple. You don't have to have the same financial arrangements in later life as you had when you were younger.

We often see widows whose husbands had cash and investments scattered all over the place. It was confusing, it caused tax problems, it made no money, and it was often expensive.

So set aside time now to discover what your financial arrangements are and tidy everything up. Simplify your accounts and investments, and make sure everyone who needs it has access to funds.

Our top tips for managing your finances in your later years:
- Get financial advice from someone who specialises in later life finances — don't try to do it all yourself.
- If you're married or in a couple, make sure there's money in each person's name so you have access to cash if you need it.
- Set aside some money in an emergency fund, to take

care of unexpected expenses.

- Take expert advice to make a will that suits you and your family circumstances.
- Put a lasting power of attorney in place to ensure your financial and personal welfare is taken care of if you lose the ability to make decisions for yourself.
- Make sure you're claiming all the benefits you're entitled too, especially when you're going into care.
- Don't pay tax you don't need to! Most people don't have to pay the tax they pay when they're older, but they don't get the right advice.
- Document all the money you have, and make a note of where it is.
- If you have private health insurance, and you can afford to keep it, do so! Premiums can get quite high the older you get, but you're more likely to need it as you get older. The NHS is great, but you might want to create a health fund just in case you want to have something done faster than the NHS can do.

Above all, remember: you're not alone and you don't have to try to deal with everything alone. Get advice from someone who'll be able to help you secure your future and enjoy your later years.

Finding an Expert

Financial planning is important at any stage of life, but never more important than in your later years. After you've retired, your income is more-or-less fixed. There'll be no pay rises, no bonuses, and no more career opportunities.

But that doesn't mean living a life of frugality.

With the proper planning and great advice, you can make the most of your money and even grow your income. You can make sure your future is secure, put money aside to enjoy your later years, and leave something for your family's future.

But who do you turn to?

Recommendations from friends and family are often a good place to start.

Make sure whomever you choose is a Chartered Financial Planner. Look for an accredited financial planner through the Society of Later Life Advisors (SOLLA), because they specialise in working with older people.

You can search on the SOLLA website for an advisor in your area:

www.societyoflaterlifeadvisers.co.uk

Lynne Gadsden from Grovewood Wealth Management Ltd specialises in wealth management and financial planning for later living and has worked with us to write this chapter.

Lynne advises that it's really important you work with someone whom you trust. Someone who'll take the time to get to know you, your family, and your circumstances. She says, "Start planning as soon as possible — before you retire if you can. You'll give yourself the absolute best chance of having a comfortable, fun retirement without any worries about your future care. But if you're already retired, it's not too late! Get in touch with a specialist later life financial advisor as soon as possible.

"The saddest stories I hear are of those who never take any advice at all, and don't do any planning. They're the ones who struggle in their later years, at a time when they should be enjoying life. So don't put it off. It could mean the difference between joy and hardship.

"Before you make any decisions on your future finances, talk to an expert who'll be able to help you decide what's best for you based on your individual circumstances."

Summary

- Fewer than three in ten people at retirement age have any plans to fund their long-term care — our government can't afford to take care of everyone, and the ageing population is only going to exacerbate the problem.

- With some careful planning and some expert advice, you can make sure you have enough money not just for the essentials, but also to enjoy your later years and leave something behind for your family.

- Make sure you're claiming all the benefits you're entitled to, and that you're making the most of the money you have.

- You don't have to sell your house and spend all your money on your care — by planning carefully and with professional help, you should be able to ring-fence the money that goes into your care and use the rest in any way you please.

- Consider putting an independent funeral plan in place to cover your funeral costs — that way, you don't risk your estate falling short, and your family won't have to find large sums of money while they're grieving.

- Get specialist advice on what to do with your pension — there are lots of options, and it's a complicated area.

- Avoid leaving too much money to the taxman by doing some careful inheritance tax planning — covered in Chapter 4 — most people pay far more than they need to.

- Start planning now! And get expert advice because it's never too early to secure your future.

In Chapter 3, we'll look at pensions. There are many different types of pension, and many options for drawing it when you do retire. It's important to get professional advice — and Chapter 3 will help you do so.

Your Notes

Chapter 3

What About Pensions?

Pensions are a crucial part of lifetime financial planning, but they're often overlooked. The best time to start paying into a pension is as soon as you start working — the sooner the better. But late is better than never, so if you've never saved into a pension before — or you're worried you might not have enough for your retirement — read on.

That's what this chapter is all about.

Let's start by cutting through all the jargon surrounding pensions and look at what they actually are.

A pension is simply a tax-efficient way to save for your retirement. It will provide you with a source of income when you stop working.

As you work, you pay either a regular amount of money into your pension pot, or you can pay in lump sums. Your pension provider invests the money for you, and your investment (hopefully) grows. Then, when you retire, you have a pot of money to enable you to start taking an income as a substitute for the income you had when you were working.

You might be wondering if you really need to think about personal pensions at all. After all, there's a state pension, isn't there?

Well, yes... and it's a good basic safety net, but for most of us it won't be nearly enough.

As of April 2018, the new state pension was £164.35 per week or £8,546 per year. Does your current standard of living match that income — even taking into consideration fewer outgoings in retirement? For most of us, the answer is "no".

Unless we make extra savings, we're going to have a shortfall and we won't be able to live the lifestyle we want to when we retire.

With a growing and ageing population, the Government is having to make changes to make sure it's still able to pay a pension at all, so the state pension has changed quite dramatically over the years. The retirement age moved from 65 to 67, then again from 67 to 68 — and it will almost certainly rise again in the future because we're now living much longer, healthier lives.

But if you're anything like me, you'll want to choose to retire when you want to, not when the Government decides you should. Putting a personal pension in place gives you that choice. And it will give you a higher standard of living if you plan well.

Experts think we're at a crisis point already with pensions. The average pension size in the UK is about £50,000, which isn't really an awful lot of money when you consider it may have to pay you an income for 20 years or more. Later in this chapter, you'll see just how far that £50,000 will go (or, rather, how far it won't go).

Start Saving Early

A common question is: when should I start saving for my pension?

The answer is: as early as possible.

The more you contribute when you're young, the bigger your pension pot will be, and the less stressful it will be later on. It's also a good idea to get into the habit of saving as early as possible. We'll look at some calculations later in this chapter.

Auto-enrolment (which we'll look at in a moment) has made it much easier for young people to start paying into a pension fund, but what about older people?

What can you do if you're aged 45 years or over and only have a small or no pension?

Start by looking at where you are now. Get in touch with a financial advisor, and take a look at your current situation.

How much are you paying into a pension at the moment, and how much can you afford to pay in?

If you're able to increase your contributions, you should definitely do so.

And consider alternatives to a pension, too: property, ISAs, and other savings accounts are all options for you.

One common reason people are reluctant to pay into a pension is you can't access it or use it until you're at least 55 years old (rising to 57 years old by 2028), which means you can't access your money if you need it. If that's the case for you, look at other options — for example, an ISA, which will give you access to your money earlier if you want or need it.

Hopefully, though, more and more people will start saving early — and auto-enrolment is making this much easier.

Auto-Enrolment is Changing the Way We Think About Saving

People are finding, more and more, that they're reaching age 65 and thinking about retiring — but they simply don't have the funds to do so.

In response to this, the Government introduced automatic enrolment in 2012 to help more people save for later life through a pension scheme at work.

In the past, many people have missed out on valuable pension benefits, either because their employer didn't offer a pension, or because they simply didn't apply to join the company pension scheme.

Auto-enrolment has made a big difference already to the numbers of young people saving for a pension early. It makes it compulsory for employers to automatically enrol their eligible employees into a pension scheme — and the company must also pay money into the scheme.

If you're aged 22 and earning more than £10,000 a year working for an employer, you'll be automatically enrolled in a pension scheme. All eligible employees in the UK should now be automatically enrolled into a company pension scheme — and I strongly advise you to stay enrolled.

Nobody wants to think about retirement when they're young. I didn't, when I was first starting out. The idea of me at retirement age was like a different planet. Young people tend to live for today and let tomorrow take care of itself. And there are other priorities when you're younger: the average age to buy your first house in the UK is now around 30-35, so people are thinking more about deposits than saving for old age.

Auto-enrolment has done a lot to help people prepare for retirement, but contribution rates are still too low.

Contributions are set to go up to eight percent on qualifying earnings — which may sound like quite a big chunk of your income, but it's not much of a contribution.

For example, if you're earning £15-£25,000 per year your pension contribution is only based on around £9-£19,000 of that income… and although eight percent is better than nothing at all, it's still not very much. We're likely to see auto-enrolment contributions go up in future, but you can do something about your own pension now.

Let's take a look at how much money you'll want to retire on, and how much you can contribute to your pension before you do retire.

How Much Can You Contribute?

I asked David Allen, a chartered financial planner at 2h Wealthcare LLP, how he helps people plan for the future and how much money people should contribute to their pension funds. He uses cashflow modelling with his clients, and always starts by asking people what their plans are for when they retire.

So I'm going to ask you to do the same here. Answering these questions is a good place to start:
1. When would you like to retire?
2. What would you like to do when you stop working?
3. What kind of an income would you like to have from your pension?

When you have a good idea of what you want your retirement to look like, you'll be able to start making proper plans for your future.

David uses a lot of visual aids like graphs to demonstrate to people that they'll have enough to do what they want when they retire… or that they certainly won't have enough as things stand now.

How much you'll pay into your own pension scheme will very much depend on your lifestyle. We're all different and we all have different expectations of what our retirements will look like. The best advice is to pay in as much as you can afford from as young an age as possible.

You want to provide for your future — but you also want to make sure you don't adversely affect your standard of living and lifestyle today. It's all about striking the right balance.

Let's look at some figures.

If you want an income of £5,000 per year when you retire aged 65, here's how much you'll need to start paying at different ages:
- At 25 years old, you'd need to pay £269 per month.
- At 45 years old, you'd need to pay £501 per month.
- At 55 years old, you'd need to pay £947 per month.

So you can see, the sooner you start saving for your pension and the more you can put away, the better.

At the other end of the scale, you might be wondering how much you're allowed to put into your pension.

The laws have changed over the years and will probably change again in the future, but at the time of publication you can pay up to £40,000 a year or 100% of your salary (whichever is lower) and the Government will give you tax relief on that contribution.

Not many people actually do pay in that much to their pension, though.

You should also be aware that if you're a high-earner and make more than around £110-£150,000 per year, you might not be able to get tax relief on the full £40,000. If this applies to you, make sure you get professional advice before you make any decisions.

What Types of Pension Are Available?

If you work for a company as an employee, there are two main types of pension you may be enrolled in or allowed to join. If you're self-employed, you also have options. And saving for retirement isn't just about pensions… you do have other options, too.

Defined Benefit Scheme

Also known as "final salary pensions", these gold-plated schemes are very rare today. They're calculated on how many years service you have with your company.

Each year you gain a year's service, then when you retire you receive a percentage of your final year's salary as a pension payable for the rest of your life. It's also inflation-proof. Most schemes are not open to new members now — as you can imagine, they're very costly for employers.

Public sector workers and teachers still have access to a watered-down version of the defined benefit scheme, called a career-averaged scheme.

Defined Contribution Scheme

Most people are members of a defined contribution pension scheme — also known as "money purchase" schemes. You pay a percentage of your salary into a pension scheme. The money is invested for you, and the pot grows.

Then, rather than a guaranteed income, you choose how to take an income from the pot when you retire. It's very different from the defined pension scheme.

Self-employed

If you're self-employed you can set up a personal pension for yourself privately. Personal pensions are the same as defined contribution pensions: your pension pot will hopefully grow over years of investing then, when you retire, you get a choice of options.

Lifetime ISA

The Lifetime ISA was introduced in April 2017. It's for people aged under 40 — and if that's you, you can pay up to £4,000 a year into it. The Government gives you tax relief on that £4,000, so you get a bonus of 25% annually — which means your £4,000 becomes £5,000.

The Lifetime ISA was designed for first-time home-buyers and enables you to withdraw your money without penalty and retaining tax relief to buy your first home. There are limits on the value of the property you can buy, but it's a very good way for people looking to buy their first property to get an additional incentive and cash from the Government.

Or, you can leave your cash where it is and then draw it aged 60, like a pension plan or bank account without penalty. However, like an ordinary ISA, you can only put £4,000 per year into a Lifetime ISA.

Salary Sacrifice

If you're making contributions to a company pension scheme,

the company might offer you the option of "salary sacrifice". You and your employer may make a legal agreement to reduce your earnings by an amount equal to your pension contributions.

In exchange for reducing your earnings, your employer then agrees to pay the total pension contributions (from you and from your employer) into your pension scheme for you.

For example, if you're earning £30,000 per year and you pay £2,500 per year into your company pension scheme, you can choose to give up that £2,500 as part of your salary instead. Your new salary would now be £27,500 per year, enabling you to save money on income tax and National Insurance contributions. Your employer will also save money on NI contributions and may rebate some of those savings into your pension plan.

If you choose to take part in salary sacrifice, it will affect your terms and conditions of employment and is a matter of employment law, not tax or pensions law.

Most people choose to take home the same net pay but increase their yearly pension contributions. However, you could choose to increase your net take-home pay and contribute the same (lower) amount into your pension scheme.

Salary sacrifice can be a good option for lots of people. But give it careful consideration, because reducing your basic salary may affect any benefits you're entitled to.

It may also affect whether or not you get a mortgage. If you reduce your salary, your lender may not give you the mortgage you hope for. Most mortgages are now decided on affordability rather than salary, but it's a good idea to get professional advice before you make any decisions.

Pensions Are Not Your Only Option

Although a pension is an absolute must, it's not your only option. It's never a good idea to put all your eggs in one basket, so you might want to consider other investments for your retirement, too.

Investing in real assets, like property, forestry, and gold, are a good idea too. They're tangible.

Buying property and investing in buy-to-let properties can be a very good way to produce an income, but there are associated risks. For example, if you're unlucky enough to get poor tenants, you may find yourself without a rental income for a while.

Some of the tax advantages of owning buy-to-let properties are decreasing and some people with huge portfolios are starting to reduce those portfolios.

You may also want to look at commercial property, ISAs, or stocks and shares, depending on your willingness to take risks. There are lots of investment options available, and many of them work well with a pension as part of your overall retirement plan and portfolio.

Some people invest in art, rare books, or classic cars — but those are quite volatile markets, and regulated investments are definitely safer. If you want to invest in something more unusual, definitely get advice from a specialist in that field.

The best advice is to put a diversified portfolio of investments together to spread the risk, rather than put all your eggs in one basket.

Whatever you decide to do, getting advice from a professional is very important.

The Tax Benefits of a Pension

If you're still not sure whether or not a pension is a good idea, consider this: for tax purposes, a pension is the best possible investment you can make to save for your retirement. You've already paid tax on the money you put into your pension, so the Government gives you tax relief on those contributions as you pay into it.

For example, if you contribute £100 per month to your pension, the Government will give you back the tax you've already paid on it. So you'll only pay £80 from your bank account because the Government gives you back 20% in tax relief.

And if you're a high-rate taxpayer, you can claim an additional 20-25% back during your self-assessment.

If you work and are enrolled in a company pension scheme, the company has minimum contributions they have to make too. So you get tax relief from the Government and money added to your pension pot from your employer, too.

A company pension is the best investment you can make. Think about it this way: if you invest £1 and your company invests £1, you'll have £2 invested — but it'll only cost you 80p! Where else are you going to invest 80p and get a £2 return without doing anything? That is a fantastic investment.

Your pension fund will also grow tax-free. You won't be charged income tax on the money you've invested, and it's not subject to capital gains tax, either.

When you retire and decide to draw your pension, you can take 25% of the value of your pension pot as a tax-free lump sum. So, if you had a pension pot of £100,000 you could take £25,000 immediately tax-free. After that, the income you take from your pension is taxed at your marginal rate, however you decide to take it.

A pension is a very good inheritance tax tool, too. Pensions fall outside your estate so if you don't need to use your pension, it's a great way to pass wealth down to your spouse or children. You can leave your pension to any person or to a charity if you don't have children.

Just make sure you complete a death benefit nominee form to give instructions to your pension provider as to where to pay the funds when you're gone.

When You Retire

When you retire and you're ready to draw your pension, you have a couple of choices. Up until April 2015, most people bought an annuity. When you retired, your provider would look at how much you have in your pot, then write to you and offer to swap your pot for a lifetime income.

Most providers sent out an offer for a single-life annuity, which gave the highest income — but people didn't realise they had a choice. Most accepted the single-life annuity because it gave more money — but they didn't realise it was only payable to them. So if they died early, they wouldn't be able to pass on their benefit to a surviving spouse or anyone else.

The Pension Freedoms Act of 2015 gave us all much more choice about how to access our pensions as we wish from the age of 55. It's led to more people wanting to invest in a pension because they're now much more flexible.

Perhaps you have £100,000 in a pension pot, and you want to take £25,000 as a tax-free lump sum, for example. Then, you could choose to take all the rest of the money straight away. Or, you could choose to take £1,000 this year, nothing next year, and £5,000 the year after.

You now have much more flexibility about taking an income from your pension plan.

Taking an annuity is the right choice for some people... especially if you're in poor health because you may be entitled to a higher level of income. But the choice is now yours.

"What happens if I want to draw down a lump sum on retirement?"

If you want to take a lump sum when you retire, you can. You can take your 25% tax-free lump sum, then you can take the rest of the pot as a lump sum too if you want to.

Be very mindful, though: if you do that, the lump sum is added to your year's income.

For example, if you take £75,000 as a lump sum, you'll pay high-rate tax on that income. It's a very good idea to spread it out over years if you can. But if you want or need the whole sum sooner, you can split it over two years: taking half on April 1, and half on — for example — April 7 to spread the tax over two tax years.

If you do take your pension as a lump sum, be aware you'll have to do some tax-wrangling: it will probably be treated as a "month 1 earning" for tax purposes, which means HMRC will assume your lump sum is a monthly income and tax you accordingly for the rest of the year. You'll be able to claim it back later, but make sure you get advice so you don't get any nasty surprises.

"Will my pension pay for social care later on?"

Another thing to keep in mind is social care if you need it later in life.

When the authorities look at how you pay for social care, they look at all the assets you have. If you leave your pension pot untouched and don't take an income from it, when you get to pension credit qualifying age the local council will assume you're receiving an income from your pension even if you're not.

The council looks at how much you have in your pension pot and works out from an annuity rate how much income you'd receive if you were drawing your pension. They take that figure as the amount of money you're receiving as an income and will offset pension funds against the cost of social care.

This is why it's so important to plan for your future carefully — there are many pitfalls waiting for the unwary.

Working in Retirement

Lots of people choose to carry on working beyond retirement age. If you earn enough money from your work, you won't need to draw a pension — and you can carry on growing your pension pot until you do need or want to retire.

Some people decide to work part-time and take some of their pension to top up their income. Pensions are very flexible now, and you can work out what you want to take to fit your lifestyle and cover all your wants and needs.

It's similar for business owners. Business owners often don't "retire", they carry on doing what they love to do. But pensions are a great way to get money out of the business and into a pension fund — saving on corporation tax. Pensions are good for extracting profit from the business in a tax-efficient way.

When you pay yourself a salary or dividends, you pay income tax and dividend tax on those incomes. But paying money into a pension means you can gain corporation tax relief on that money.

Retiring Overseas

Many people decide to retire overseas... and who can blame them? The weather is much warmer in many parts of the world! Or perhaps you have family who've relocated abroad, and you want to join them.

If that's the case, you can still take your pension benefits as a UK resident. You can choose to take a lump sum or regular income. Do speak to an international tax specialist, though, because the income you take may be taxed in a different way from the UK. You can still access your pension fund, but make sure you know how it'll be taxed in your new country of residence.

You may decide to transfer your pension abroad, depending on where you go. Lots of Australian ex-pats have moved their pensions over there because tax benefits are better. But do get advice from a specialist so you know exactly what you're getting into, and so you can plan properly for your future.

Choosing a Pension Scheme

Choosing a pension is a bit like going to a library to read a book. You know you want to read something, but you're not sure what. With all this choice, how do you choose?

You do have several options when it comes to choosing a pension — and your best option will depend very much on your circumstances.

It's a very good idea to get help from an independent

financial advisor (IFA). Think of it as an investment rather than a cost, because a good pensions specialist will help you make the most of your money and savings, and could mean the difference between a comfortable and fun retirement, and struggling after you stop working.

Financial advisors have comparison tools at their disposal that will look closely at your individual circumstances: how much you want to invest, your age, and how much risk you're prepared to take with investments. The advisor will use this information to research the best option for you.

IFAs are not tied to any single provider or pension type, and they're not allowed to take commission from pension providers anymore either. They truly are independent. When you work with a professional, they do all the hard work and analysis for you, and you have the benefit of years of their experience working with investments.

Or, you can take advantage of the online tools available to you. Many pension providers will take you through a decision tree process, which asks you questions designed to find out about your lifestyle, income, and how much risk you're prepared to take. Then they'll suggest a suitable investment and pension plan. It does make it easier to choose, but it can still be a bit of a minefield.

And any pension provider's decision tree is only going to help you choose between their options, so it's not really impartial.

It really is worth working with a professional. You might be worried about the fee — but you have options there, too.

You can agree on a fee and pay your advisor up front — or you can fold the fee into your pension payments for the first year. The advisor gets paid the fee via your pension provider, so you don't have to pay the lump sum straight away.

It works a little like a mortgage arrangement fee — the arrangement fee is added to the mortgage itself, so you pay it off gradually.

Choosing An Independent Pension Advisor

Word of mouth is definitely the best way to find a good financial advisor. If you have friends or family who've worked with someone who's done a great job, it makes sense to talk to their recommendation.

If you don't have any recommendations, though, start with Unbiased.co.uk, which is a great website. You put your details in, explain what you're looking for, and the website will recommend three local advisors.

There are several things to consider when you're choosing an independent financial adviser:

- What type of advice are you looking for? Is it just to choose a pension, or do you want help with all your financial planning for retirement?
- Check how much experience your chosen advisor has — are they a pension specialist?
- Does your chosen advisor look after clients who are similar to you?
- Will you be dealing with one dedicated advisor — or will you be dealing with several people? It's much better to find one person you can trust.
- Check what they recommend: do they recommend products from the whole market or just a small number of providers?
- Make sure you understand their fees and that you can afford to pay them.
- Always check your advisor is authorised to give financial advice. You can check they're registered with the Financial Conduct Authority (FCA) Register at https://register.fca.org.uk/.

A good financial advisor can make a huge difference — not just to your standard of living, but to making your financial planning much simpler and easier.

I asked David about how he's helped a recent client. Here's his client story:

"A client aged 47 came to see me last year because he was concerned he wasn't paying enough into his pension plan. He was worried he wouldn't have enough money to retire when he wanted to. We sat down together and discussed his personal circumstances so I could understand how much he had in savings and pensions and what his retirement goals and needs would be.

My client had built up a reasonable amount in his pension pot through his employment and was a member of the company scheme — and he told me he'd like to retire on an income of £22,000 per year at the state pension age of 67. Would his current pension pot allow him to do so?

By using a cashflow forecast and assumptions based on how much risk he was prepared to take with his investments, we calculated that he'd be okay until his 83rd birthday — at which point there'd be a shortfall. His £22,000 per year would run out.

To provide a guaranteed income, my client decided he would buy an annuity when he reaches age 67. It suits his risk profile and means he won't have to worry about income in the future.

We planned for him to take the tax-free lump sum to provide additional capital to bridge the shortfall in his income. He will also be entitled to a full state pension, so we included that in the calculations, too.

Then we looked at how much excess income he had and how much he could increase his monthly contributions by. We cashed out some of his other investments and invested half into his pension and the other half into a new ISA. By making these changes we showed he would have sufficient funds to provide the income he needs until age 90.

We've made an agreement with our client to provide an ongoing service, so we'll be reviewing his investment funds each year to check we're still on track to meet his income objectives in retirement. If anything changes, we'll know straight away and we can make plans to deal with any problems before they arise."

The last thing you want is to get to retirement and realise you simply don't have enough money to live the life you want. Even worse, is getting to a ripe old age and suddenly running out of money entirely.

Good financial planning with an expert will help make sure you're well prepared for your retirement and old-age — so instead of worrying about money, you can be enjoying yourself.

Summary

Start investing in your retirement as young as you possibly can! The average UK pension pot is just £50,000 — and I hope you now realise that's not really going to give you much of an income when you retire.

The earlier you can start and the more you can pay into a pension, ISA, or other assets, the more choice you will have for your retirement.

Start thinking now about what you want and when you want it. For most younger people it seems a million miles off and most people don't start paying until they think they have enough money to do so. By then it's quite late and things can be much trickier.

- A pension is simply a tax-efficient way to save money for your retirement, so you can replace your working income with a pension income when you stop working.
- If you're auto-enrolled into a pension scheme with your employer — stay enrolled! And contribute as much as you can afford without plunging yourself into hardship today.
- Don't put all your eggs into one basket: consider ISAs, property, and other types of investment to spread your investment risk.
- Get professional advice when you're choosing a pension — and also when you're getting near to retirement age. You want to make the most of your money, and avoid paying tax you don't need to pay.

- Get into the habit of saving early... and if you have children who haven't started planning yet, give them a copy of this book!
- Don't rely on the state pension alone to give you everything you need: it will not be enough for most people to enjoy the lifestyle they would like to live.

In Chapter 4, you'll discover how to plan for inheritance tax. Most people pay far more than they need to, so it's worth getting professional advice. It could save you (or your children) a small fortune!

Your Notes

Chapter 4

Planning For Inheritance Tax

Inheritance tax has been around since before the French Revolution, and it's very controversial. It was introduced to try to redistribute wealth for the benefit of all. Without it, you perpetuate inherited wealth, so the children of the rich remain rich. There's an argument to be made in its favour... but ultimately, the money is taxed at the time it's earned, so is it really fair to pay tax on it again?

Leaving politics aside, most of us would rather our wealth went to our families or charity, not HMRC.

Unless we're very careful, our families could end up paying a lot of money to HMRC in inheritance tax.

There was a time when inheritance tax was meaningless to everyone but the very wealthy, but that's no longer the case. If you own your own home, your estate may well be larger and wealthier than you might think.

If your taxable estate exceeds the Nil Rate Band, you may have to pay tax on it. The Nil Rate Band will be £325,000 until

2021.

In the period ending May 2017, HMRC collected £5.1 billion in inheritance tax. Much of that went to the Government needlessly. But inheritance tax is a voluntary tax, so with careful planning and professional advice, you can avoid it altogether, even if you have a lot of assets. Your assets include:

- Cash in the bank
- Investments
- Any property or business you own
- Vehicles
- Payouts from life insurance policies
- Pensions

Some assets are taxable, some are not. Some pass under a will, some do not. Some might qualify for relief from inheritance tax, others won't.

Transactions you've made in your lifetime are sometimes brought back in when you die, so how inheritance tax is worked out can be quite complicated.

Generally, the first £325,000 of a person's estate is tax-free. Married couples or civil partners can leave behind a taxable estate worth £650,000 tax-free. Above this threshold, tax is charged at 40%. If you leave at least 10% of your estate to a charity, the tax rate on the rest of your estate reduces to 36%.

During the 2017/18 tax year, a new "residence" allowance was introduced. It is complicated but generally is only valid on a property the deceased once lived in and where the beneficiary is a direct descendant (this includes children, step-children, and grandchildren).

The basic allowance of £325,000 each stays the same. This is what you get on top of that:

- For the tax year 2017/18 it starts at £100,000 (giving a total allowance of £425,000), rising by £25,000 each year until it reaches £175,000 (giving a total allowance of £500,000) in 2020.
- For the tax year 2017/18, the maximum you can pass on

tax-free is £850,000 for married couples or those in a civil partnership, and £425,000 for others. For singles, this includes the existing £325,000, plus the extra £100,000. For couples, when the first one dies their allowance is passed to the survivor, so that £425,000 is doubled to £850,000.

- In 2020, the tax-free amount will rise to £1 million for couples (made up of £325,000 x 2 plus £175,000 x 2) and £500,000 for singles (made up of £325,000 plus £175,000), as the residence allowance increases.
- On estates worth between £1 million and £2 million, 40% inheritance tax will apply to the amount above the tax-free amount.
- On estates worth £2 million or more, homeowners will lose £1 of the "residence" allowance for every £2 of value above £2 million. So for a couple, estates worth £2,350,000 or more will get no additional allowance at all.

People in certain "risky" roles don't have to pay inheritance tax if they die in active service or from an injury sustained whilst in active service that ultimately causes their death — even if they die years after being injured. Risky roles include those in the armed forces, police, firefighters and paramedics, and humanitarian aid workers.

If someone injured on active service dies early because of the injury, they are also exempt from inheritance tax, even if they're no longer on active service.

If you're married, any assets you leave to your spouse or civil partner when you die are exempt from inheritance tax. And your partner's inheritance tax allowance increases by the amount of your allowance you didn't use.

If you're not married to your partner, things get much more complicated and you should definitely get specialist advice when making your will.

I'm sure you'd prefer your assets to go to your family, rather than the Government, when you die — so what can you do to protect them?

Well, you can do a lot to reduce or even eliminate inheritance tax — but many people don't do anything.

Reducing Your Inheritance Tax Bill

You can give money away before you die, but it's usually counted as part of your estate, so if you die within seven years of giving the gift, your estate and possibly the person who received the gift will have to pay inheritance tax (IHT) on it.

A gift must be genuine and unconditional, and you can't get it back. A big mistake many people make is thinking they can give away their home, but continue living in it — unfortunately, that doesn't count unless you pay market rent to the new owner.

Many gifts are perfectly valid ways of reducing the inheritance tax bill, but you must be careful.

Planning to live longer is all very well, but there are no guarantees. However, there are other ways to cut your tax bill:

- You can give away £3,000 a year tax-free (and you can carry it forward for one tax year if you don't use it this year).
- You can leave money to charity tax-free.
- You can give gifts of £250 to any one recipient per tax year, tax-free.
- If you have excess income from a pension or earnings, you can give that away tax-free, as long as it doesn't affect your lifestyle.
- You can give away gifts in consideration of marriage tax-free (up to a maximum of £5,000 from a parent, £2,500 from a grandparent, and £1,000 from anyone else), but you have to give the gift on or just before the wedding date and the marriage must go ahead.
- If you own a farm, other agricultural property, or woodland, a percentage of it may be exempt from inheritance tax.

- You can write life insurance policies and pensions in trust so they're not included in your estate when you die.
- You can set up a trust which gives you control but which starts to leave your estate for IHT after seven years.
- You can set up a trust which gives you a lifetime income while the capital leaves your estate for IHT after seven years.
- You can create a later life trust, so your investment grows and the capital leaves your estate for IHT but still provides you with an income when you need care.
- You can take out an insurance policy that pays the inheritance tax for you, so your beneficiaries receive more.
- Put a good pension in place, because pensions aren't included in your estate for inheritance tax, if managed correctly — but make sure you complete the death benefit nomination form, so you can leave your pension to your loved ones.
- You can invest in products which qualify for business or agricultural property relief so no, or less, IHT is due on death — if you've owned them for two years.

Inheritance tax is a complicated area, and if you have any kind of substantial estate you really should get specialist advice.

Finally, keep in mind that planning to avoid inheritance tax is important, but not at the expense of your own financial security and fun! It's great to leave gifts to children and family, but don't sacrifice everything for someone else's future. You've worked hard for your money and you deserve to enjoy it.

Planning for Inheritance Tax

You can create massive tax savings by drafting a tax-efficient will. If a married couple have both been widowed and they leave everything to each other, to then pass down to others, there is no inheritance tax on the first death. On the second death, the first £650,000 is free of inheritance tax. But if the first to die creates a certain trust in their will instead, they may each be able to leave gifts of £650,000 to others, tax-free — a saving of £260,000.

If you leave property to children, you may be able to claim an extra inheritance tax allowance — but if you haven't taken advice and/or if your will isn't drafted properly you may not know what options are available and you may lose out.

For example, you wouldn't want to leave a house to a charity and give cash to the children.

If you own your own business, you'll need to set out in your will what you want to happen. For example, you could put powers in your will to give executors the ability to carry on the business and wind it up as a going concern, so it's worth more for your beneficiaries. If you don't allow this in your will, your executors may not have the authority to deal with it — and the assets could lose value.

Without a well-drafted will, you can lose value on your assets because your executors may not have the power to deal with complex estates right away. You can also create a trust as a way to reduce your inheritance tax bill.

A trust is a way of managing assets. A little like a limited company, a trust is its own legal entity and owns assets like property, money, or other investments. Trustees of the trust look after those assets as a nominal owner on behalf of others (the beneficiaries).

Trusts affect different taxes in different ways, and you should get specialist advice about it. But inheritance tax is the big one, and it's the main place you can make savings.

We've acted for clients to mitigate their inheritance tax by using trusts on many occasions. The client who stands out most was a lady who owned several large properties in central London. The properties were settled in several trusts to benefit her children and grandchildren, which removed the property from her estate but ensured her family benefited from it after her death.

Tax planning and trust work are very complicated, but this example is a good illustration of how significant your tax savings can be if you plan properly. Our fees weren't small, but they paled in comparison to the several hundred thousand pounds of inheritance tax we helped her to save.

Trusts can be incredibly useful and also incredibly complicated, so if you think you might want to set up a trust you'll definitely need to get specialist advice. To find out more about trusts, read Chapter 6.

Summary

- If your estate exceeds the Nil Rate Band, currently £325,000 until 2021, you may have to pay tax on it. Remember, if you own your own home, your estate may be larger than you think — so do get professional advice.
- With careful planning and professional advice, you might be able to avoid IHT altogether — even if you have a lot of assets.
- Your pension is not included in your estate and is not subject to IHT if dealt with correctly — so a pension is a tax-efficient way of saving for retirement and leaving an inheritance for your loved ones.
- There are many ways to reduce inheritance tax bills in your own lifetime, including giving away gifts to family and charities, creating life insurance policies, and creating trusts.
- A well-drafted will can sometimes help you save thousands of pounds in inheritance tax, as well as making life simpler for your loved ones after you're gone.
- It's well worth getting professional advice about your finances if you want to avoid paying inheritance tax needlessly.

In Chapter 5 we ask the question, "Do I really need a will?" and go through how important making a will is. You'll also read about the common pitfalls, and how to avoid them.

Your Notes

Chapter 5

Do I Really Need A Will?

"I leave all my Manchester United memorabilia to my beloved wife, and the rest of my estate to my neighbour, Brian.

"No, wait… that's not right!"

You may smile, but that's what actually happened to a client of one of our solicitors some years ago. Her husband had made a DIY will using a pack from a high-street shop — and had made a perfectly innocent mistake.

Thankfully, the neighbour immediately agreed to reject his inheritance and change the will — but had he not, our client could have faced a lengthy battle to inherit.

That's an amusing anecdote, but making a will is incredibly important — even if you don't think you have much of anything to leave.

According to research conducted in 2015 by Prudential and Unbiased.co.uk, nearly 60% of adults in the UK haven't written a will — leaving their final wishes in the hands of the Government, and risking their estates going to people they might not want to benefit.

Around a fifth of people believe they're not wealthy enough to need a will, but if you own your own home you're probably worth more than you think.

The average homeowner has more than £214,000 worth of property — but only 32% of people aged between 35 and 54, those most likely to have dependent children, have written up a will.

Without a proper, well-thought-out will, it's unlikely your final wishes will be carried out the way you would want. And the Government may take a larger portion of it than is necessary.

Before we go into what happens when you die without a will, though, you might be wondering exactly what this legal document is.

Put simply, a will is a document — usually written — which deals with most of what you own when you die.

Most people will have a written will — but it is possible for some people to have an oral will. Those going on active military service have a little extra leeway from formalities, but it's always best to put it in writing if you can.

All sorts of terms are bandied about when it comes to wills. Here are the most common three you may hear about.

Mirror wills are virtually identical documents created for two people, in which they leave their estate, usually to each other, in the same way. The most common format is everything to each other, and on the second death, to the children. Each person has their own will, though, so it's really no different from a "normal" will.

Mutual wills are quite rare and complicated. This type of will creates a binding agreement between two people which aims to prevent the survivor from changing their will and disposing of the estate in a different way.

There are generally better and simpler ways to achieve those aims, though — for example by making a normal will including a life interest trust. If you think you may have a less straightforward will, it's very important to get professional advice.

Finally, you may have heard the term "living will". These specify what you'd like to happen to you if you're alive but mentally incapable, for example with medical treatment decisions. Making an LPA (lasting power of attorney) is usually a much better option because it gives you more flexibility.

Do You Really Need a Will?

If you're not rich and you don't have a big collection of gold, jewels, or art, you might be thinking you don't really need to make a will. After all, your situation is fairly simple.

But if you own your own home, you probably have much more wealth than you think.

Whatever the size of your estate, though, making a will ensures there's someone to sort out all your affairs, administer everything, and make sure your wishes are granted. It will make life much easier for your family and loved ones.

If you die without a will — which is called "dying intestate" — the Government decides who gets what from your wealth, referred to as an estate. Your spouse or civil partner is first in line, but won't necessarily receive everything. Next in the queue are children or grandchildren, parents, siblings or their children, half-siblings or their children, grandparents, uncles and aunts or their children and, finally, half-uncles and aunts or their children.

If you have no relatives, your estate passes to the Crown or the Duchies of Cornwall or Lancaster. All of these rules are known as the laws of intestacy.

So, as you can see, if you die without making a will it's entirely possible some (or all) of your wealth could go to people you don't know very well — or at all.

Some time ago, an unmarried couple who had been together for more than 30 years came into our law firm. They didn't have children but were shocked to discover that if one of them died their assets wouldn't go to the other partner. They had thought the "common law wife" concept would protect them. No such concept really exists in UK law.

Because each person owned everything in their individual names all assets would have passed to their respective families. And because the property they lived in was solely in the man's name things would have been particularly difficult if he died first. Under the intestacy rules his estranged brother would have inherited the house — and they had no idea where he was. The partner wouldn't have received any part of the property. She would have had to make a claim against the estate.

This couple only needed simple wills — but what a difference they make. Now they're both protected.

If you are married, your spouse automatically gets priority — but if you've been married before, or have children from a previous relationship, that may not be what you want. Without a will, you can't be sure your assets will go where you want them to, especially if there are step-children and multiple marriages.

The other problem with dying intestate is there's no executor. The law decides who administers your estate, but that person won't have the same powers as someone you appoint yourself.

The court-appointed administrator will need to get a grant from the court before they can legally do anything with the estate to make sure they don't face any unnecessary liability, and that can take time. Even dealing with personal items gets tricky without a will and an executor. People may want to start dealing with your possessions straight away, but an administrator doesn't have any authority to do that. Even giving away clothes to the charity shop has to wait. Everything almost grinds to a halt without the proper paperwork.

If you appoint your own executor by making a will, that person has authority from the day you die, so all your affairs can be dealt with more quickly and more easily.

It's sensible to make plans for what might happen, even if your assets would go the same way under intestacy rules. If you have a will, everything will be very clear, and you'll be able to appoint an executor to sort out all the paperwork.

We also find many people change their minds about what they want when they get specific advice. What seems simple at first may turn out to be more complicated than you might think — for example, what if you have children, and your spouse remarries? Can you be sure your children will be looked after? If you get a professional to help you, you can be sure your wishes will be complied with.

What to Consider Before You Start

It's a very good idea to book a consultation with a solicitor or will writing professional to talk about your circumstances and what you want to do with your estate when you're no longer with us.

Before you do so, there are a few things to think about:

- What do you own — what's included in your estate? Consider property, land, vehicles, and personal items of value.
- What will happen to your vehicles? They can be awkward to deal with, so dealing with them in your will can be helpful for your executors.
- Whom do you want to benefit from your will — whom do you want to leave your worldly goods to?
- Who do you trust to be the executor of your will?
- What will happen to your children, if they're under 18? Who do you want to look after them?
- What about pets?
- What funeral arrangements would you like to make? What type of burial?
- Do you know what your beneficiaries might have to pay in inheritance tax — and do you have arrangements in place to minimise any taxes? (More information on inheritance tax in Chapter 4.)
- If you have your own business, will that keep running?

Try to think practically about what might happen after you're gone. Who holds keys for your property? Does anyone know where all your paperwork is? If your solicitor is the executor of your will, who will tell your solicitor about your death?

When someone has no children or close relatives, they often come to us for help with how things might work. If you're in a similar situation, you don't have to think about all this alone — professional help is available.

But even if you do have a family, it's a very good idea to at least talk to a specialist solicitor before drafting a will — they can help minimise any inheritance tax, and make sure your wishes are clear and complied with.

How to Make an Effective Will

In an absolute emergency, you could, in theory, scrawl your last will and testament on the back of an envelope... but we don't advise it!

If it's not written clearly and well, it may not do its job at all.

In this section, I'll run through a few simple tips and examples so you can make sure your will is valid and does what you need it to do.

At the very least, you must make sure it's written legibly and that it's dated and signed in the presence of two witnesses. If you have an attestation clause — a short statement that the will has been signed by the person making it in the presence of two witnesses who have also signed in the presence of each other and the person making the will — that will help move probate along.

You might think signing your will is obvious, but you'd be amazed at the number of cases we see where people simply forget to do so, or do it wrong.

Here's a quick tip for making probate go more smoothly: when your witnesses sign your will, ask them to print their name, address, and occupation underneath to make it easier to find them.

You don't have to date your will — a missing date won't invalidate it — but it does make probate a little more difficult.

Make sure your will is easily understood, too. Not just that it's legible, but that it makes sense. You could have a perfectly valid, legible, signed and dated will — but if it's waffly or unclear, and doesn't deal with certain assets well, it can lead to uncertainty.

And uncertainty can lead to arguments.

For example, you may want to leave your entire estate equally to your nieces and nephews... but what if one of them died before you? Where does their share go? If there's no substitution clause, it could lead to a partial intestacy if it isn't written correctly. One of our clients had this problem — complicated by the fact that their family was scattered all over the world.

I started this chapter with the story about the man who wrote his own high-street will and accidentally left his Manchester United memorabilia to his wife, and his worldly goods to his neighbour. You may think it's obviously a mistake, and of course it is — but the fact that our client's husband didn't mean to write his will like that doesn't matter under the law. It was written very clearly, it was signed, and it was dated. His will was legally binding.

The neighbour agreed to vary the will, which you can do if you have the capacity, and if you do it within two years of death it can be read back for certain tax purposes, too — but if the neighbour had refused to cooperate or couldn't cooperate, it could have gone to a full court case. The widow would have had to apply for the will to be set aside, which would have been costly and time-consuming.

Another classic mistake people make is creating a seemingly simple will — something like, "I leave my house to my son and the rest of my assets to my daughter". It seems simple — until the house is sold before death and the proceeds from the sale go into the cash pot, so the daughter gets everything.

When assets are sold and turned into cash, the cash beneficiary can receive more than the dead person intended.

Another common problem is mentioning a specific asset in their will — but by the time the person dies, they no longer own that asset.

Or owning shares in a company which has since changed its name.

The will won't be effective unless there's a clause that allows for changing names and disappearing assets.

This is why it's so important to phrase your will very carefully — and why it's so important to get professional help.

A solicitor will be able to explain all this to you and ensure your will is drafted in such a way that it's as tax efficient and clear as possible.

I want you to be able to think and plan your will as effectively as possible, which is why I'm including this information and these examples... but it's no substitute for getting professional help.

How to Change a Will

You can change a will, and there are certainly circumstances in which you'd want to change it.

Many people don't realise the implications of marriage and divorce. If you get divorced, the will isn't revoked, but it does treat the ex-spouse as if they'd died. If you marry without a contemplation clause, then on that marriage your will is revoked and your new spouse will take priority — which may not be what you want if you had children from a previous relationship.

We had a married couple as clients, who had made their wills with us. They were just finalising their divorce, but had a very good relationship and still wanted to leave everything to each other for the sake of their children. They didn't want to tie everything up in a trust and make things complicated — they trusted each other still and just wanted to keep it simple. So they wanted to make new wills to ensure they could still leave everything to each other, and look after the children in this way.

You might want to consider changing your will if you buy a house abroad, or otherwise acquire some foreign assets. If you're British, your will here will deal with everything you own in the UK — but it usually won't deal with property owned elsewhere. If you own property in France, for instance, you'll probably find it easier to have a French will as well as a British one. It's usually best to have a will in each country, but they must be compatible.

If you make a will before you have children, you may want to alter it after children come along to make sure they benefit, and perhaps to add a guardian clause to say who'll take care of them. Or you might want to put the money in trust so the children can't touch it until they're, say, 25 — rather than inheriting it aged 18.

Many people ask if they need to change their will every time they buy something valuable — and the answer is generally no. That would become tiresome and expensive!

If your will is written in general terms and you have a straightforward estate, you can simply leave your assets generally and distribute them as you wish.

If you do get more assets, or buy a second property, you should definitely revisit your will — if for no other reason than to make sure as little as possible goes to the taxman.

Dealing with personal items can be long-winded — and rather than change your will constantly, you can simplify things with a personal chattels clause that leaves your personal items to your executors and asks them to dispose of your belongings in accordance with wishes set out in any attached letter. You can update the letter as you wish — but do make sure you choose executors you can trust as the letter is not legally binding.

If you think you might want to change your will, the best thing to do is book an appointment with your solicitor. Bring in a list of your assets, and think carefully about your wishes.

Making a Will for Someone Else

If someone loses mental capacity before they make a will, you can apply to the Court of Protection for a statutory will.

You can apply to do this when the person isn't able to understand:

- What making or changing a will means.
- How much money they have or what property they own.
- How making or changing a will might affect the people they know (either those mentioned in the will or those left out).

If you want to change a will, you'll need to provide a lot of evidence to support your application, including the following information:

- The current will.
- A draft of the new will.
- Information about powers of attorney.
- Information about the executors.
- The family tree.
- Details of all beneficiaries.
- Your reasons for applying to change an existing will.
- Set out the person's beliefs and values and explain their past actions, so you can show they would make these changes themselves.
- Inform everyone involved that you're applying to the Court of Protection.

If you're applying to create the first will, you'd basically need to provide all of the above, plus what the intestacy decision would be according to the current situation, and what you're proposing instead.

Remember, someone who has lost the mental capacity to manage their finances may still have the ability to make a will. Your solicitor will be able to advise you.

Keeping Your Will Safe

The best place to keep your will is in a locked, waterproof, fireproof safe. You can also ask your solicitor to store it for you — we store our clients' wills for them free of charge.

You can keep it in your bank, but they tend to charge you for the service.

If you use a will writer, ask them to confirm their fees and what happens if the will writer closes their business. You need to be sure your will can easily be found should you want to update it, or on your death. On occasion, we see clients whose wills have got lost and we were unable to trace the person who originally drafted it. Our clients had to make new wills.

Solicitors are regulated by the Solicitors Regulation Authority which means you're protected. If your firm of solicitors closes down, they usually send their will bank to another solicitor and the Solicitors Regulation Authority keeps records. So if you lose track of your will, or you forget to give your new address to a solicitor, you can always contact the Solicitors Regulation Authority and follow the paper trail.

It's not compulsory to register a will, but if you're not storing it with your solicitor, it may be a good idea to do so.

Getting Professional Help

Having the wrong type of will could have huge repercussions for your family and loved ones. You may be reluctant to spend the money on a solicitor, which is understandable — nobody wants to think about these things…

But think of it as an investment for your family's future.

It's what you don't know that's the problem — even if your estate looks straightforward on the surface.

For example, perhaps you and your partner own your home as joint tenants, which means the house will pass automatically to your partner outside your will on your death. But if you want to leave your half of the house to your children, you'll have to change the way you own it and put the appropriate clause in your will.

Your will won't work if you don't understand the implications of what you write.

And perhaps the most persuasive argument for getting a specialist solicitor to draft your will is this: inheritance tax. At the time of writing, generally any estate worth up to £325,000 is free of inheritance tax. For any assets over and above that threshold, estates can be taxed at 40%. You may not think your estate is worth that much, but when you combine property, vehicles, and other assets it all adds up.

If your estate is larger, you'll definitely want to think about inheritance tax: can you write your will in such a way that you minimise the amount of tax due?

Perhaps.

But a specialist solicitor will definitely be able to do so. In fact, they may be able to save your beneficiaries many times the solicitor's fees.

Here's an example from a recent client. Her estate is worth quite a lot of money and she wanted to leave £50,000 to charity. But doing so would mean the rest of her estate was over the tax-free allowance, leaving her estate with a big tax bill. We structured her will in such a way that she left a little more to the charity — 10% of her estate — which meant the rest of her estate was taxed at only 36%, rather than 40%. Her beneficiaries received just about the same amount they were going to receive before, but with less money going to the taxman.

Paying a few hundred pounds to arrange a will now could save thousands of pounds in tax for your beneficiaries in the future.

Another good reason to go to a solicitor is that your solicitor is under a duty to make sure you're not being unduly influenced by someone else, or coerced into making a will you're not happy with.

Solicitors aren't your only option for arranging a will. You could go to a professional will writer. If you do so, check they're regulated and insured, and make sure they're qualified. Will writing firms are not regulated by the Solicitors Regulation Authority, so there are fewer safeguards. But if you do decide to use a will writing firm, check they're members of the Institute of Professional Willwriters, which has a code of practice approved by the Trading Standards Association.

Solicitors are highly regulated, so if you choose to engage a solicitor you'll be protected by the Solicitors Regulation Authority. If you do choose a solicitor, make sure they're a member of STEP, which shows they're specialists in writing wills and dealing with estate planning.

Many solicitors will offer a free initial consultation so you can discuss your circumstances and find out if there's anything specific you need to think about.

A free consultation will also give you the chance to get to know your solicitor, which is really important. After all, you're leaving your final wishes in the hands of someone else, so you want to make sure it's someone you like and trust.

What Are Your Circumstances?

If you're still not sure about whether or not to get professional help, I'd like to tell you a few client stories that may help you decide.

Eliminating Inheritance Tax

Some time ago, an unmarried couple with two children came to see us at our offices. They had no wish to get married but they each held assets worth approximately £320,000 and no property, so they had a combined estate of approximately £640,000.

They recognised they'd need wills to be able to leave everything to each other on one of their deaths but hadn't realised the tax disadvantages of doing this. On the first death, nobody would have to pay tax on the assets of around £320,000 passing from one of them to the other. But on the second death, the combined estate would pass to their children — and that would total around £640,000.

The survivor would only have access to one set of inheritance tax allowances. At current tax rates, if the second partner were to die in 2018, the tax bill would be £126,000. That's a lot of money going to the taxman when, with proper planning and wills, it could be going to their children.

We created discretionary trusts in their wills so that one would come into existence only after the death of the first partner. This way, they could leave their estate so the survivor could benefit from the assets, but wouldn't inherit the estate outright. On the second death, the inheritance tax bill for the children would be zero.

What might seem like an expensive solicitor's bill is just a tiny fraction of that £126,000 inheritance tax bill.

Taking Care of Children

On another occasion, we were instructed by a married couple with children aged 8 and 6. Their estates would pass to each other, then to the children in equal shares without a will. But they were shocked to discover the children would be entitled to a large inheritance once they reached the age of 18. By writing wills, they could increase the age of inheritance to 25. They could also appoint executors to deal with the administration process, appoint guardians for the children, and their executors as trustees would look after the funds until the children reached aged 25.

Without wills, the children would inherit everything aged 18 — and the couple's choice of guardians would not be clear.

Taking Care of Elderly Spouses

Another lady came into our offices concerned about her husband, who suffered from Alzheimer's. She had been diagnosed with a life-limiting condition and was probably going to die before he did.

She was anxious to make sure she protected her husband's position and provided him with an income — but also wanted to protect the capital value from her half of the house for her children. Her husband would need to move into care, and if her half of their house passed to him entirely, it would potentially all go to pay for his care and diminish their children's inheritance.

We wrote into her will a life interest trust to help make sure everyone was taken care of.

Children from Previous Relationships

If you have children from previous relationships, things can get complicated when it comes to inheritance. Without a will, your new spouse will take priority, and your own children may not receive anything.

We had a married couple as clients, both of whom had children from previous relationships. They each wanted to make sure they left something to the surviving spouse, including the right to stay in their home. But they also wanted to ultimately provide for their own children.

Without wills, the survivor would have inherited everything, and the children of the second to die would inherit the entire estate — excluding the first-to-die's children entirely. With wills containing the appropriate trusts, they were able to achieve a balance, and protect all the children as they wished.

Leaving Money to Charity

If you have a little wealth and you want to make the most of it, an effective and well-drafted will is important. One of our clients was a wealthy lady who wanted to leave her estate to various charities and her extended family — and she wanted it to be as tax-efficient as possible. She had a homemade will listing several specific amounts to go to charity, with the rest going to family. Her will did achieve what she wanted — but it left her family with a high inheritance tax bill.

By changing the way her will was written, and leaving 10%

of her estate to charity so she could benefit from a reduced rate of inheritance tax, we reduced the eventual inheritance tax bill by more than £200,000. That £200,000 went to charity instead, and the family received only a very little less than they were previously inheriting.

Complicated Assets and Families

If your estate is complex and you have challenges within your family, you'll definitely want to get professional help with writing your will.

Just like a wealthy gentleman who came to our offices. He wanted to appoint professional executors because of his complex assets but didn't feel his family, who had difficulties, would be able to handle his estate when he died.

We were happy to help, and at the same time put his affairs into an order that would make it as easy as possible for the firm to administer when the time came. We made sure the papers were all in the same place, we had details of who to contact and the man's funeral wishes, and we were able to advise on inheritance tax to make sure his beneficiaries received more than they would have before.

For example, we made sure life assurance would pay directly to his beneficiaries, rather than going via the will. This reduced the inheritance tax for that portion of the estate to zero.

We recommended financial advisors to help him invest some wealth in assets that qualify for business property relieve, so after two years they wouldn't be subject to inheritance tax. And he was able to find other reliefs he could use, such as annual and small gifts, and gifting excess income to give away money without incurring tax. All this helped to reduce the estate value so less inheritance tax would be payable on his death.

Summary

Without expert advice, most people are unaware of how they can reduce their inheritance tax bill enormously, and make sure their families and beneficiaries benefit rather than the government.

Do consider getting professional help to make your will. Many solicitors offer a free initial consultation, so you can talk with them and find out what your options are and what are the implications of doing it yourself.

- Wills aren't just for the super-wealthy — the average homeowner has an estate worth at least £214,000. Without a will, it may not be distributed the way you'd want. A simple, well-drafted will can put you at ease.

- If someone loses mental capacity before they make a will, you can apply to the Court of Protection for a statutory will. You'll need to do plenty of research and set out your arguments as to why what you're proposing is the best thing to do.

- Choose your executors carefully, because it's a big responsibility and can involve a lot of work on their part if your estate is large or complicated.

- Before you start drafting your will, consider some basics — starting with what you own. Consider property, land, vehicles, and any personal items of value.

- Think carefully about whom you want to benefit, whom you trust to be the executor, and whom you want to look after your children or pets.

- Creating a trust can save tens of thousands of pounds if you have a large, wealthy estate — or a trust can ensure children or disabled beneficiaries are looked after for the rest of their lives. Get specialist advice about trusts, because they're very complicated areas.

- Be very sure your will is effective and does what you want it to do. The best way to be sure is to work with a specialist solicitor, who'll help you avoid any pitfalls.

- If your personal circumstances change significantly, or you acquire more property or wealth, consider changing your will to reflect this so everyone knows where they stand.

- Keep your will in a locked, waterproof, fireproof safe, or ask your solicitor to store it for you. If you're not storing your will with a solicitor, consider registering it with the National Will Register.
- It's a very good idea to get professional help drafting your will, even if it's only a simple will. You'll be sure everything is in order, and there'll be little chance of any confusion or uncertainty arising after you're gone.

I've mentioned trusts several times in this chapter, so in Chapter 6 I'll go into more detail about what trusts are and when you might want to consider setting one up.

Your Notes

Chapter 6

What's a Trust and When Should I Use One?

A trust is a way of managing assets. A little like a limited company, a trust is its own legal entity and owns assets like property, money, or other investments. Trustees of the trust look after those assets as a nominal owner on behalf of others (the beneficiaries).

They can be incredibly useful and also incredibly complicated, so if you think you might want to set up a trust you'll definitely need to get specialist advice.

There are several different types of trust with varying levels of complexity. In this section, we'll deal with the most common types.

Life Interest Trust

Life interest trusts are fairly common when families join together. For example, if a couple with previous children gets married or lives together, they might each want their own children to benefit from their half of their property. In that case, you'd set up a trust in the will so when one spouse dies, the other spouse can live in the property for the rest of their life, then on the second death the house is divided and left to the children on each side.

This type of trust provides assets for the next generation but provides a benefit for the surviving parent.

Lifetime Trust

You'd set up a lifetime trust to be active in your own lifetime, rather than in your will. You may want to do this if you have very young children and want to put money aside for them until they're old enough to look after it themselves.

Because the trust is its own legal entity, that money would no longer belong to you — it would belong to the trust until the children came of age.

You may find there are tax advantages to setting up this type of trust.

Will Trust

A will trust enables you to leave property or money to someone who isn't yet of age. You can set aside the assets to hold in trust until they reach the age you specify.

Discretionary Trust

A discretionary trust could be a lifetime trust or a will trust, but it gives trustees wide powers to decide what they want to do with the assets or money. The beneficiaries do not have a fixed entitlement or interest in the trust funds.

Instead, the trustee has the discretion to determine which of the beneficiaries will receive the capital and income of the trust, and how much each beneficiary is to receive. This is a very flexible option if you want to leave property or money to "all of my descendants", for example.

There are many, many options if you're thinking of setting up a trust, and many reasons why you may want to do so.

Trustee Responsibilities

Trustees have a legal obligation to look after the trust's assets in the best interests of the beneficiaries, in accordance with trust documents and with general law.

For example, trustees have a duty to invest money properly, to take advice where necessary, and to take advice from beneficiaries about their needs.

Trustees must also do tax returns for the trust if it's subject to income tax or capital gains tax. If it's a more complex trust, there may be other charges and responsibilities, too.

You must ensure you have enough trustees to run the trust. How many you need will depend on the type of trust you're setting up.

Keep in mind there are heavy penalties if trustees don't live up to their responsibilities or maintain the trust properly. If mismanagement means the trust loses value, beneficiaries have the right to sue for the amount lost. For example, if a big trust was sitting on a current account instead of being invested wisely, the beneficiaries can sue the trustees.

And if there's any suggestion of fraud, it could be a criminal offence.

If you want someone to act as a trustee for your trust, bear in mind they have a right to refuse. It's a good idea to talk to potential trustees in great detail about their responsibilities, so everyone goes into the arrangement with their eyes open.

Why Create a Trust?

If trusts are so complicated, why not just leave property and money in a more straightforward way? People are motivated to create a trust for a huge range of reasons, but the four most common motivations are:

1. To have the trustees control the assets within the trust rather than the beneficiary

If you're setting up a lifetime trust, you might make yourself the trustee.

If it's a trust set up for after you die, your trustees might be the executors of your will, or perhaps your solicitor.

An obvious example where this is a good idea is if a parent or family member dies and leaves money or property to children who aren't old enough to deal with it themselves. In this case, you'd set up a trust in the will and set the age of entitlement appropriately — perhaps you'd choose for your children not to be able to access the money until they're 25.

Or perhaps you want to control what happens to a property you own. You can settle it into a trust with rules as to how the property is run and managed in the future. In this way, the property becomes its own legal entity. Your trustees can control what happens to it, what happens to any income, and decide how and when to sell the property.

You can leave land to a charity on the condition it's only used for certain purposes — or you can put it into a trust.

If a property you own has been in the family for generations, and you want to keep it in the family for the long term, you can leave it in trust for several generations. This way, there's no risk of an errant child selling it — he can't do so because it's not his to sell.

2. Flexibility

If you have a large family or want to leave your estate to many beneficiaries, you can leave your assets in trust for the trustees to control. They can decide who benefits depending on their circumstances.

This can be very helpful for families with lots of children and grandchildren. If you know they'll need it at some point, but you're not sure who'll need what, when, and how much a trust can take care of all that for you.

3. For Tax Purposes

You might want to leave money or property in trust for tax

purposes. It can be very tax efficient for wealthy people to settle some money into a trust during their lifetime to avoid paying a hefty inheritance tax bill.

One of our clients was very wealthy and had several properties in London. Most of them were held in lifetime trusts and the trusts benefited from the (very high) rental income. When she died, this arrangement saved her beneficiaries an enormous amount in inheritance tax.

Remember: you can find out more about how to minimise inheritance tax in Chapter 4.

4. Looking After Disabled People or Children

Trusts aren't solely the preserve of the rich, though. Leaving your assets in trust can be the perfect solution if you have young children or disabled dependents who can't look after the money themselves.

One of our clients had a disabled child who was just about to reach the age of 18. They wanted to set up a trust for him, enabling him to live as independently as possible in sheltered accommodation in the future, and giving him a nest egg for the rest of his life.

If they'd just given him money, he wouldn't have been eligible for government help with housing and care, and he would have struggled in the future to provide for himself. This was a practical way for our clients to help their disabled child for the rest of his life, and ensure he has enough money to live on.

Trusts Aren't For Everyone

Unless you have a specific reason (such as disabled children), it's not usually worth setting up a trust for an estate worth less than £250,000.

"How do I set up a trust?"

In short: you don't! You get an expert to do it for you because the implications of getting it wrong are huge. The tax implications alone can be enormous. We've also seen clients who've set up trusts themselves without realising they can never get the money back personally. Once it goes into trust, you no longer own it — so be very sure about what you want to achieve, and get advice before you do anything.

Another good reason to get expert advice is the rules surrounding trusts and taxes are obscure. You might want to set up a range of different trusts for tax reasons — but how much tax you save (or pay!) will depend on when and how you set them up.

The type of trust you may need will depend very much on what you want the outcome to be. So before you start talking to anyone, decide what your goal is in leaving assets to beneficiaries, then get expert legal advice to help you achieve the goal.

You may also find you don't need a trust at all: we often have clients come to us to say they want a trust — but when we talk to them we find they don't need a trust to achieve what they want to do. It's possible to do it in other, much simpler and less expensive ways.

Who Can Help?

For anything other than the very simplest trusts, find a solicitor who specialises in them and isn't a generalist.

Go to a firm with a good reputation, and with solicitors who have plenty of experience. This is a complex area of law and you really do get what you pay for. There are many, many pitfalls for the unwary and inexperienced, and the tax implications can be huge.

Talk to your chosen solicitor, make sure you trust them and make sure they have the experience you need.

See if you can find a firm which offers a free consultation, and go prepared. Make a list of your assets, note down what you want to achieve, and explain your situation. During the free consultation, you'll be able to find out if a trust is the best option, and if it is, whether you want this firm to act for you.

Summary

- The most common types of trust are: life interest trust, lifetime trust, will trust, and discretionary trust. But there are very many other options too, and it's best to get professional advice if this is something you're considering.
- Trustees have a legal obligation to look after the trust's assets in the best interests of the beneficiaries.
- Make sure you have enough trustees to run the trust — this will depend on the type of trust you're setting up.
- The main reasons for setting up a trust include: putting assets under the control of trustees rather than the beneficiary, flexibility, for tax purposes, and to look after disabled people or children.
- Unless you have a specific reason (such as disabled children), it is not usually worth setting up a trust if your estate is worth less than £250,000.
- The tax implications of getting trust work wrong are huge — so definitely find a professional who specialises in trust work.

In Chapter 7, we'll go through the practicalities of what to do when someone dies. Bereavement is already a very difficult time, so having a good idea of what you need to do will help enormously.

Your Notes

Chapter 7

What To Do When Someone Dies

When someone dies, you're not just dealing with bereavement and grief. There is, unfortunately, a lot of official paperwork that needs to happen. One of those things is probate.

You might be wondering what "probate" means — and you're not alone. We get a lot of questions about it. In its simplest terms, a grant of probate is the legal document which gives permission for those named as executors in a will to deal with a dead person's estates and assets.

It gives you the legal right to carry out all your duties as an executor.

Not every will needs a grant of probate — if you have only a very small and simple estate worth less than £5,000 (sometimes a little more), you may be able to simply write to the bank or whomever is holding the money, and ask if they'll make a payment without a grant of probate.

To apply for probate, you complete form PA1 and the relevant Inheritance Tax form.

Once you've filled in the forms, send them to the local probate registry together with:

- An official copy of the death certificate.
- The original will, plus three copies.
- The fee (£215 at time of writing, or £200 in Northern Ireland).

If you're in Scotland, contact your local Sheriff court for the forms. The procedure will depend on the value of the estate. In Northern Ireland, contact the Probate Office to arrange an appointment.

When you apply for a grant of probate (or confirmation in Scotland), ask for sealed copies (50p each at time of publication) for asset holders (banks, insurance companies, etc.). You cannot use photocopies.

When funds are released, pay everything into the executor's account. The executor can then pay the legacies plus any interest if this happens one year after the anniversary of the death.

Before you apply for a grant of probate, you'll have to pay any inheritance tax due.

It's a good idea to engage a specialist chartered legal executive or probate solicitor to help you with this, because they will fully understand the terms of the will.

There are many things that can complicate probate, such as complex trusts, and schemes designed to allay inheritance tax.

If you want to pay as little inheritance tax as possible — and most of us do! — you must consider getting professional advice. Chapter 4 will give you more information about minimising inheritance tax.

A solicitor will make sure you fill in all the forms correctly, and advise whether you may need more complicated forms for more complex estates.

Professionals can also give you many valuable tips to help you avoid penalties of inheritance tax, valuations, shares, and cash assets. A professional can save you many times their fee, so think carefully before trying to do it all yourself. We recently saved a client more than £300,000 in inheritance tax which they would almost certainly have had to pay, had our client taken the DIY probate route.

A common pitfall for people trying to do it themselves is tax. If an estate has inheritance tax due, there are strict deadlines to meet — and the penalties are stiff. It can take much longer than you'd think to get valuations done and get the paperwork in order, especially if the deceased's records are untidy.

If inheritance tax isn't paid within six months of the date of death, interest is added from the end of the month in which the death occurred. And there are hefty penalties for declaring incorrect property values — for example, if you make an estimate, or sell to family at a lower-than-market value.

There's an awful lot to think about, and it has to be correct and on time. The authorities don't care if it's a genuine mistake — ignorance of the law is no excuse. As an executor, you're liable for the penalties.

If you do decide to work with a probate solicitor, choose a firm with a separate private client department. Solo solicitors can be great, but they can often be generalists when you really need a specialist.

The right firm may well be different from the ones who dealt with the will.

Local knowledge is useful, too — a solicitor local to the deceased person will have good contacts, will know local estate agents and other organisations, and will know who to ask for help with the specifics of administering an estate.

Other organisations do offer probate services, such as banks and some accountants. But probate may not be their speciality.

Before any of that, though, you need to make sure you have a will — and not just any will, but one that clearly communicates your wishes.

The chapter on making a will tells you everything you need to know about making an effective will. But what happens with your will after you die?

What Does An Executor Do?

Being asked to be the executor of someone's last will and testament is flattering — after all, it's the final act of trust. But you may be wondering what's involved in the role.

It can involve a lot of work and responsibility, which could go for months — even years. So if you're asked by a loved one to be executor, think carefully about whether you're willing and able to fulfil the role.

If you're thinking about writing your will and considering who to appoint as executor, make sure you tell them exactly what's involved. Even better — give them a copy of this book!

In short, an executor is someone named in a will who'll handle your estate (your money, property, and possessions) after you die.

You can name anyone you like, and you can choose up for four executors so they can share the responsibility. You can even choose someone who will inherit from your will.

An executor's main duties are to:

1. Secure and preserve the deceased person's assets after death (the executor should check property is insured, remove any valuables from the home, and do anything else that's needed to keep the estate safe).
2. Value the assets and establish the liabilities (find out how much each part of the estate is worth, and find out whether there are any debts owed) in order to obtain a legal document called a Grant of Probate.
3. Organise payment of inheritance tax (if any is due).
4. Once you receive the Grant of Probate, send a copy of it to any organisations holding the deceased person's assets, such as their bank, so assets can be transferred to the executor's account.
5. Pay any outstanding taxes and debts.
6. Distribute the estate to those who benefit from the Will.

Ultimately the executor's aims are to identify the estate's assets and value them at the date of death, deal with all the deceased's debts and outstanding payments, and distribute the inheritance to those entitled to it.

Executors can claim expenses from the estate for the work they do, and a solicitor can help, too. Getting professional help is a good idea if the estate is particularly large or complicated.

If there are relatives, they will almost certainly register the death themselves. If there are no relatives, the executor may register the death if they're also arranging the funeral.

You don't have to tell the family doctor, although if you can find it, it's a good idea to give the deceased's medical card to the Registrar, who'll send it to the Primary Care Trust to update their records.

Think about how many copies of the death certificate you'll need because it costs less to ask for them when registering the death than if you need more later. Be aware that nobody — individuals or solicitors — is allowed to photocopy death certificates under Crown Copyright Law. Asset holders like banks will always require an original death certificate.

If you're employing a solicitor to take care of the estate, you won't need to worry too much about this. If you're administering the estate yourself, you may need a copy for each asset holder — companies like insurance providers, landlords, mortgage companies, banks, and the TV Licensing company.

Next, you'll need to find the latest version of the will. Always try to find the original if you can.

If you really can't find the original, you can use a copy as a last resort but you'll need to get permission from the Probate Registry. The executor will need to provide the court with an Affidavit of Search to confirm they've searched all the paperwork, checked with all local solicitors, and searched anywhere else the original will may be located. The executor will also need to confirm this copy is the last will as far as they are aware.

If there are other executors, you need to get confirmation they're happy for you to hold the original will.

Make copies of the will for co-executors and beneficiaries. Keep the original in a safe place and don't alter it in any way — not even to add staples or paper clips. This is really important because if it appears the will has been tampered with at all, it could cause legal problems later on.

More Practicalities

As executor, you might find you're the one responsible for arranging the funeral. If so, check the will to find out if the deceased person had any specific funeral wishes. If they had a funeral plan, contact the plan provider straight away.

Tell family, friends, and any colleagues about the death and consider putting a notice in the newspaper with details of the funeral so people can attend if they want to.

The executor is also responsible for valuing the estate. You'll need to look at everything they owned at the time they died, including money, property, and possessions. Then subtract everything they owed like mortgage, credit card bills, and loans.

HMRC recommends having any items worth more than £500, including property and land, valued professionally.

You may also find yourself looking after the deceased person's property. If it's not occupied, make sure it's secure and tell the insurance company immediately. They'll tell you what to do next.

You can contact the Bereavement Register at www. thebereavementregister.org.uk and put a Royal Mail redirection to the executor's home in place to stop post being delivered. You can go to the local post office with a death certificate and your ID or post it to Royal Mail. There is a fee, but you can claim it back as an executor's expense.

Redirecting mail is the best way to make sure no assets are missed because most financial institutions send an annual review at the very least.

When it comes to finances, you'll need to send an original death certificate to banks, building societies, and insurance companies so you can cancel direct debits and standing orders. Ask for final account balances and investment values at the date of death.

You'll also have to stop any salary, pension, and state benefit payments. Inform credit card companies, the passport office, the DVLA, and the TV Licensing people of the death, and follow their instructions.

Find out if you can use the Tell Us Once service to cut down on how many government departments you have to get in touch with. Not all councils use it, but if yours does it could save time.

It's very important to find out about any debts the deceased person may have had, and any overpayments made to them. Go through all their paperwork looking for bills and statements, and contact utility companies and the local council to check if any money is owed.

If you go through all the finances and think there might be more debts than assets, the estate may be insolvent and you'll need to get professional help before you do anything else.

You'll need to find out if any tax, like income tax, is owed by the deceased person.

You may find it helpful to open an executor's account if your bank offers one. You can transfer any money paid into the estate there, so there's no risk of your personal money getting confused with the estate's money.

Before you do anything else with the finances, you must pay any outstanding taxes, debts, and bills. You can't legally distribute the estate to beneficiaries if there's still money owed by the estate.

Get clearance from HMRC for any inheritance tax, income tax, or capital gains tax.

It's a good idea to put "statutory notices to creditors" in the press, allowing two months and one day to make a claim against the deceased's estate. If you don't do this, you (and any other executors) will be personally responsible for any claims arising after the time limit expires.

The notice goes into the local paper where the deceased lived (or more than one place if they owned more than one property) and into the London Gazette. It costs around £160-£200. Professional executors must place statutory notices. If the executor is a family member, it's not always necessary to do so.

Once you've made sure there's nothing owed, you can distribute the estate.

If the will states a specific personal item should go to someone, you can give it to them before probate is granted — but make sure you get it valued first.

Once probate has been granted you can create estate accounts for each beneficiary. They should include all the assets you've collected, any income accrued, and any bills you've paid.

Distributing the Estate

Before you distribute any wealth, you'll have to carry out bankruptcy searches on each beneficiary. If someone is bankrupt, they may not be entitled to receive their inheritance. You can carry out searches on the Individual Insolvency Register.

Read the will carefully, and distribute the estate according to what it says. If there is any money left to children aged under 18, it can go to parents or guardians if the will gives permission and it's practical to do so. Otherwise, any gifts will have to be held by trustees. If this is the case, make sure at least two trustees have been named.

If there's the slightest possibility of someone making a claim against the estate, do not distribute it for at least one year from the grant of probate. Although the statutory period for making a claim is six months from grant of probate, when that time limit draws near any claimant can apply to bring a claim out of time, which means the statutory period will increase.

When we have clients in this position, we always advise them to wait until a year has passed just to be on the safe side.

Even if you're sure there will be no claims, it's a good idea to wait at least six months after probate is granted, just in case someone makes a claim against the estate.

When you do distribute the estate, give each beneficiary a tax form for their share of income arising from the estate since the date of death. Keep records of what you've done so you can easily show how you got from the value at the date of death to the value at distribution. This will also help you answer any questions or challenges about how you've administered the estate.

The estate is also subject to income and capital gains tax. You may wish to consider getting professional help to work through the paperwork in the most efficient way possible, so you can avoid capital gains and income tax where you can.

For example, if an executor sells a property themselves this will come under a single capital gains tax allowance, which means any tax payable may be considerable. Instead, the executor could deed the property to beneficiaries, so they can each use their own capital gains tax allowance when the property is sold. This may reduce the tax payable considerably, or even avoid it completely.

You will definitely need a grant of probate to sell a property. In most cases, you'll also need one to sell shares (unless it's a very small holding).

In general, probate isn't necessary if the deceased owned less than £15,000 in their sole name. However, we recently had a client who needed a grant of probate for a Government WSCC pension with a lump sum of £6,000 — so it varies considerably. The best thing to do is get advice on your individual circumstances.

Summary

- A grant of probate gives your executors permission to deal with your assets and estates after you've died. Make sure your executors know exactly what they need to do to obtain a grant of probate — or what they need to do if they don't need probate at all.

- An executor's main duties are to:
  ° Secure and preserve the deceased person's assets after death (the executor should check property is insured, remove any valuables from the home, and do anything else needed to keep the estate safe).
  ° Value the assets and establish the liabilities (find out how much each part of the estate is worth, and find out whether there are any debts owed) in order to obtain a legal document called a Grant of Probate.
  ° Organise payment of inheritance tax (if any is due).
  ° Once you receive the Grant of Probate, send a copy of it to any organisations holding the deceased person's assets, such as their bank, so assets can be transferred to the executor's account.
  ° Pay any outstanding taxes and debts.
  ° Distribute the estate to those who benefit from the Will.

Chapter 8 explains why everyone should consider putting an LPA (Lasting Power of Attorney) in place.

Your Notes

Chapter 8

Lasting Powers of Attorney and How To Use Them

What would happen to your finances and your affairs if you were suddenly unable to make decisions? It could be something serious and life-limiting, like dementia... or it could simply be an unforeseen accident or illness that puts you in hospital for weeks or even months.

One of my solicitors found herself in this situation with her parents. She arranged powers of attorney for them some time ago but didn't expect to need them for many years. Not long after she arranged everything, her mum passed away unexpectedly. Then her father had a fall and fractured his foot, and everything became much more difficult for him.

Thankfully, they had powers of attorney in place. She never expected to need them so soon, but she was very grateful to have the LPA in place because her dad doesn't have to worry about anything.

Who would take care of financial decisions and make sure

your bills are paid and your wishes carried out?

Most of us don't like to think about scenarios like this — in fact, it's not something that even occurs to most of us if we're in good health.

But it's incredibly important.

The best way to make sure everything is taken care of, so you and your family don't have to worry about things, is to put in place Powers of Attorney.

A Power of Attorney (PoA) is a legal document that allows someone to make decisions for you, or to act on your behalf if you're no longer able to make your own decisions. Or you may simply no longer want to make your own big decisions.

It's a very simple thing to sort out. You choose someone to be your legal attorney, then you (the donor), your attorney, and a third party (your solicitor, for example) sign the document.

You must have a third party to sign too, so everyone can be sure you understand the situation.

Having a PoA doesn't remove your independence and ability to make decisions entirely — if you still have the mental capacity to make your own decisions, you can do so. But if you don't want to make certain decisions or deal with certain situations, your PoA will enable you to ask your attorney to deal with it for you.

Having a PoA gives you the choice.

And it gives you peace of mind: if and when you do lose mental capacity, you'll know you have someone you trust to look after all your affairs for you.

There are many reasons you might want to put a PoA in place. It could be temporary if you're in hospital and need help with everyday things like paying bills.

Or it could be longer-term if, for example, you've been diagnosed with dementia. If you lose the mental capacity to make your own decisions in the future, you'll have someone you trust to make decisions for you.

Sometimes people may simply not want to make decisions

for themselves anymore. Their memories start to fail, dealing with finances and paperwork becomes more and more difficult, so they want to ask an attorney to do these things for them instead.

There are different types of power of attorney, and you may want to set up more than one.

Ordinary or General Power of Attorney

Putting an Ordinary or General Power of Attorney (OPA) in place allows your attorney to act on your behalf for a specific purpose or timescale, while you still have mental capacity to make your own decisions. For example, you may want to appoint an attorney to act for you in a property transaction if you're abroad, or for a specific time period, or during a temporary situation, perhaps if you're in hospital or on an extended holiday.

An OPA allows another person (or more than one person) — your attorney — to act for you for a specific purpose. You may want to set one up if, for example:

- You need someone to act for you temporarily, such as when you're on holiday or in hospital.
- You want someone to be able to access your accounts for you.
- You want someone to act for you while you're able to supervise what they do — so they're legally able to give you help without taking over.

An OPA is generally only designed to be used for a short period of time and for a specific purpose. It's important to remember an OPA is only valid while you still have mental capacity to make your own decisions.

If you want your attorney to be able to act generally on your behalf, or you want someone to be able to act for you if the time comes when you don't have mental capacity to make your own decisions, you'll need to make a Lasting Power of Attorney.

Lasting Power of Attorney

A Lasting Power of Attorney (LPA) gives someone you trust — your attorney — the legal authority to make decisions on your behalf if you lose mental capacity in the future, or with financial matters only, if you no longer want to make decisions yourself.

There are two types of LPA:
- An LPA for financial and property affairs.
- An LPA for health and welfare matters.

LPA for Financial Decisions

You can use an LPA for financial and property matters while you still have mental capacity yourself or your attorney can make decisions for you if you lose mental capacity. For instance, if you're finding it harder to get out and about to the bank or post office, you may want someone to be able to do this for you. Or perhaps you simply want someone to act for you if you don't want to make financial decisions or deal with difficult affairs yourself.

Or you can state you only want it to come into force if you lose capacity.

An LPA for financial and property decisions can cover situations like:
- Buying and selling property.
- Paying the mortgage.
- Arranging property repairs.
- Paying bills.
- Investing money.
- Making financial decisions on your behalf.

You can enable your attorney to make all decisions for you, or you can restrict what they do for you.

If you're setting up an LPA for financial decisions, your attorney must keep accurate accounts and make sure their money is kept separate from yours. You can ask for regular details of how much you're spending (or they're spending on your behalf) and how much money you have. You can ask for these financial details to go to your solicitor or a family member if you lose capacity.

If you do lose mental capacity your attorneys will automatically be able to act for you when necessary — although each decision your attorney makes on your behalf must be considered on its merits, and your attorney must help you make decisions yourself wherever possible.

LPA for Health and Welfare Decisions

This LPA can only be used once you've lost mental capacity but you need to make the LPA while you still have full mental capacity. It's for health and welfare issues, and your attorney can generally make decisions about situations like:

• Where you live.
• Your medical care.
• What you eat.
• Whom you have contact with.
• The type of hobbies and social activities you take part in.

You can also specifically allow your attorney to make decisions about life-saving treatment in your LPA. The health and welfare LPA isn't the same as a living will — but it does have a separate section for you to sign regarding life-sustaining treatment.

You'll sign both parts of the document and it's entirely up to you whether or not you give power to your attorneys to make life-sustaining treatment decisions. Without this specific power, nobody has the power to make those decisions for you, and you'll be relying on medical professionals and other institutions like carers to make the right call.

Enduring Power of Attorney

You may have heard the term EPA, or Enduring Power of Attorney. EPAs were replaced by LPAs in October 2007. However, if you made and signed an EPA before October 1,

2007, it should still be valid and effective so long as it was completed correctly and your attorneys are still living and have capacity themselves.

An EPA covers decisions about your property and financial affairs and, so long as it's unrestricted, it comes into effect if you lose mental capacity or if you want someone to act on your behalf. However, if you lose capacity your attorneys need to register it with the Office of the Public Guardian. An EPA doesn't cover your health and welfare, so it's important to think about making a health and welfare LPA as well.

If you have an EPA and want to cancel it, you can do so in either of the following ways:

- If it's not registered you can simply sign a deed revoking it, but you should make a new LPA to cover yourself.
- If it's already registered, you can apply to the Court of Protection, pay a fee of £400, and prove you still have mental capacity to revoke it (this can happen if you lose capacity through illness and your attorneys have registered your EPA for you — if you then regain capacity through treatment or recovery you may no longer want your attorneys to act for you if you have the capacity to make your own decisions).

Business Decisions

The LPA is a personal document, so if you run your own business and want to put something in place for the business, you'll need to get specific advice from a solicitor.

For business accounts, it's often a good idea to have another signatory or a joint bank account. But, again, the rules can be complicated so get advice from an expert.

What is "Mental Capacity"?

The legal definition of "mental capacity" is someone who is able to make or communicate a particular decision in question. If they don't have that ability, they legally don't have mental capacity. To have mental capacity you must understand the decision you need to make, why you need to make it, and what the likely outcome of your decision will be.

It can be difficult to decide whether someone has mental capacity because some decisions are easier than others. With early onset dementia, for example, someone may be able to decide what to have for dinner and what social activities to do — but not be able to understand and arrange their banking and insurance.

Having dementia or another medical condition doesn't necessarily mean someone is unable to make any decisions. And needing more time to understand or communicate doesn't mean you lack mental capacity. If someone has trouble communicating or understanding a decision, you should always try to overcome these difficulties to help them decide for themselves.

Just because someone is older and perhaps a little forgetful, or they choose to make a bad decision, doesn't mean they're incapable of making that decision. Ultimately, it's up to them, no matter how difficult it may be to watch.

Making decisions on someone else's behalf is always a last resort.

If a time does come, though, when you or a loved one is unable to make decisions, you'll have lost mental capacity. That's when it's really important to have a power of attorney already in place to take care of things.

Do You Really Need an LPA?

You might be wondering if you truly need an LPA — after all, it's an extra expense on top of wills and other essentials.

I'd like to answer your question with a client story. A husband and wife in their 50s came to our offices to talk about their wills. We asked if they'd considered making LPAs as well as wills, but they hadn't. They were concerned about the cost. We explained why it might be worth considering and gave them some information about LPAs and what they can do for you.

When they came in to sign their wills, they decided to go ahead and create LPAs at the same time. We registered them at the Office of the Public Guardian and about six weeks later the wife wrote to us to tell us her husband had had a stroke just after the LPAs were registered. He had lost mental capacity and a lot of physical capability as well.

She said both their lives had been utterly transformed overnight, and the one thing that made a really big difference to her life had been the LPAs. She was able to use them to help with financial provision for him now he was disabled. She'd also been able to make important decisions about his health and welfare, both of which would have been impossible without the LPAs.

She thanked us very much indeed for our advice about LPAs and said we should advise all our future will clients to put in place their own LPAs, and that we should use her as an example. I have no doubt she'll be delighted her story is in this book and helping others to have peace of mind about their future.

My advice is to think of an LPA like an insurance policy. You're insuring against being unable to make important decisions in the future. I believe it's incredibly important to ensure you and your affairs are well looked after. I also believe it's important to make sure your family can deal with everything for you easily.

Try to imagine what would happen if you were to suddenly suffer a stroke or an accident — and you could no longer make decisions. Everything would grind to a halt without an LPA. Nobody could ensure your bills were paid. Nobody could look after your financial affairs. And nobody could make health and welfare decisions for you.

The worst possible thing that happens — and it happens often — is for your family to have to stand by watching helplessly, unable to help or make decisions, because nobody will listen to them. If they're not attorneys named in your LPA, they will have no powers to act on your behalf in your best interests.

Don't assume that because you're married or in a civil partnership that your spouse can automatically deal with your bank account and pensions, and make decisions about your health and welfare if you're no longer able to do so.

They won't be able to.

Without the relevant LPA, they won't have the authority.

You're not just protecting yourself with an LPA, you're also protecting your family from a difficult legal decision-making process.

By putting in place an LPA, you're choosing who you want to make decisions for you. If you have nothing in place, the courts or social services will appoint someone — and it may not be the person you'd want to be making decisions for you.

Build your LPAs into your later living planning process. If you have nothing in place, and you do lose capacity, the only way for anyone to do anything is to go through the Court of Protection. Even your spouse or children will be unable to help you. By sorting this out in advance, you'll be making sure everyone's best interests are looked after before a panic situation arises.

One lovely client lived with her son and daughter-in-law in an annexe to their own house. Her daughter-in-law needed to sort out our client's pension and taxes. She rented out the mother-in-law's house and managed her affairs.

It was one thing to arrange for the rental to be set up. And, with her mother-in-law's help, she was able to arrange a direct debit for the rent to go into the right bank account... but that was as much as she could do. Our client was in her late 90s and becoming increasingly less mobile and less able to deal with her banks, taxes, and general financial affairs.

When we visited her at home, we put powers of attorney in place to enable her daughter-in-law to manage everything for her, so nobody had to worry.

Another client was a couple in their late 80s who wanted

to make powers of attorney so their daughters could manage things on their behalf. They were getting to the stage where they just didn't want to deal with their finances anymore — but then dad had a fall, so that made the decision for them. We put powers of attorney in place for them, and even ended up signing the documents in the back of their very small car because dad found it very difficult to get out and walk!

Later on, the dad became quite ill, going in and out of hospital. His powers of attorney meant their daughter could deal with various matters for both of them. They no longer needed to worry about financial matters, so they could concentrate on looking after each other.

There are many practical reasons for putting LPAs in place — but the peace of mind they give is priceless.

Every client we've worked with to sort out their LPAs has been extremely grateful, and everyone has been very glad they did it.

Are There Any Risks to Making a Property and Financial Affairs LPA?

By law, your attorney must do everything in your best interests. They must keep all their finances separate from yours, and be able to produce detailed records of all transactions — where your money is going, and how it's being used.

In the past, it used to be compulsory to notify someone other than your attorney that you were making an LPA. This was a safeguard, so someone else you trust could raise a red flag if they thought you were being taken advantage of at any time, or if they were worried bad decisions were being made on your behalf.

The notified person had no powers to do anything for you, but they were able to keep an eye on things and notify the Office of the Public Guardian so it could investigate any suspicions.

Unfortunately, it's no longer compulsory. The government wanted to make it simpler and easier to create Lasting Power of

Attorney documents — but it has taken away a safeguard.

This is why I always advise clients to see a specialist solicitor. Your solicitor will take you through the whole process in detail and examine any problems that may arise. They'll help to ensure your appointed attorney is capable of carrying out your wishes, and check and double-check you understand everything being put in place.

Generally, it is easy to choose attorneys if they're family — but if you have no family, who will you appoint? If it's a neighbour, do you know and trust them enough? It is a good idea to notify someone else, too, just to keep that check and balance.

A good example of something to look out for comes from one of our clients. A widow wanted to appoint all three of her children jointly and severally — which meant any one of them could do something on her behalf, but that person wouldn't need to tell the others. If that decision affected a decision one of the other children made, it could lead to confusion.

Your solicitor will be able to advise you on the best way to set up your LPAs to minimise confusion and to ensure your best interests are served.

It's a good idea to have more than one attorney as a backup in case something happens to the person who takes the most responsibility for your affairs. If something happened to your attorney — if they died, or lost mental capacity themselves — it can be very difficult to appoint someone else if you've also lost capacity yourself.

What if banks (or other institutions) won't recognise an LPA?

When LPAs first arrived on the scene, banks often struggled to understand them simply because they were new. But these days, most people know what they are — especially those in healthcare and banking.

Make sure you notify companies when you put a property

and finance LPA in place. Some of the organisations you may want to contact are:

- Banks.
- Building societies.
- Credit card companies.
- Store card companies.
- Mortgage providers.
- Insurance companies.
- Utility companies.
- Post Office.

With a health and welfare LPA, you might want to show it to your GP and any other relevant medical professionals.

Occasionally problems can crop up if they won't accept a signature or if something else doesn't quite add up. In that case, you or your attorney can get in touch with the Office of the Public Guardian, who'll be able to back you up.

If you make your LPA through a solicitor, your solicitor will be able to write to the organisation to explain the situation.

How to Object to an LPA

You can object to the registration of an LPA if you're concerned. You must tell the Office of the Public Guardian (OPG) and you may also have to tell the Court of Protection.

If you're the donor – the person making the LPA – you need to fill in the objection form LPA006 and send it to the OPG.

If you're an attorney or a "person to be told", you can make a "factual objection" or an objection on "prescribed grounds".

For factual objections, you must object within three weeks of being notified. You can object if:

- The donor or an attorney has died.
- The donor and an attorney were married or in a civil partnership, but have divorced or ended the partnership.
- An attorney doesn't have the mental capacity to carry out their duties.
- An attorney has chosen to stop acting.

- The donor or an attorney are bankrupt, interim bankrupt, or subject to a Debt Relief Order.

For prescribed objections, you'll have to provide evidence to support your objections. You can object if you believe:

- The LPA isn't legally correct.
- You don't believe the donor had mental capacity to make an LPA.
- The donor cancelled their LPA when they had or regained capacity.
- There was fraud (e.g. someone faked the donor's signature).
- The donor was put under pressure to make an LPA.
- An attorney is acting against the donor's best interests.

You then fill in the notification form LPA008 and the objection form COP7 and send them to the Court of Protection. There is no fee to object if you're an attorney or a "person to be told".

If you're not a person to be told, you can still object by filling in form COP1 and sending it to the Court of Protection. The fee to do so is currently £400.

The OPG or the COP will contact you within five days of receiving your forms.

How to Choose Your Attorneys

The person (or people) you choose as your attorney will potentially have access to your bank account and investments, be able to sell your property and be able to make decisions about your health and welfare.

You should choose the persons you trust most to keep your best interests in mind.

The whole point of making an LPA is that you get to choose the best person for the job.

If you don't make an LPA, and you lose mental capacity, the courts will appoint someone for you — and it may not be the person you'd want.

For most people, they'll appoint their spouse and their children in their LPAs. If they don't have children, they'll often choose nieces and nephews, or brothers and sisters.

Most people appoint a relative.

If you don't have any family, choose someone you trust. A close friend or professional.

When you're considering who to choose, you might find it useful to read about the five key principles your attorney must follow:

1. A presumption of capacity. Every adult has the right to make his or her own decisions. You must assume each individual has capacity to do so unless it's proved otherwise. For example, you may not be able to physically go shopping, but you're perfectly capable of deciding what to buy.

2. Support to make your own decisions. Your attorney's first responsibility is to help you, not to do it for you automatically.

3. Just because you make what may be seen as an unwise decision, you shouldn't be treated as lacking capacity to make the decision.

4. Any act done or decision made on your behalf if you lack capacity must be done in your best interests.

5. Anything done for or on your behalf if you lack capacity should be the least restrictive of your rights and freedoms.

Talk to your family and friends about what it means to be an attorney, and whether or not they feel able to carry out their duties and responsibilities. Make sure they understand that it's about helping you and supporting you while you still have capacity, not taking over. You want to keep your independence for as long as possible, and the Mental Capacity Act 2005 was put in place to ensure you can do so.

If you don't have any family or someone you trust to speak on your behalf, you can choose a professional attorney. It is more expensive, but it is an option.

Solicitors in our firm sometimes act as professional attorneys for people's property and financial affairs, because it's more of a paperwork and process task than a personal one. Making health decisions is much more difficult and solicitors generally don't do that. Doctors can make health decisions, but most don't like to do so — so generally social services will step in.

You can see why it's much, much better to choose a family member or friend you trust if you can.

Most of the time, there are no problems or concerns with LPAs — but if you do think an attorney isn't making the best decisions for you or your loved one, you can get in touch with the Office of the Public Guardian to investigate.

Or, if you still have capacity yourself, you can revoke a power of attorney at any time. You may want to do this if, for example, your daughter and her husband both have power of attorney for you, but they get divorced. You may want to remove the ex-husband from your document.

When to Create an LPA

The sooner you start thinking about an LPA, the better — in fact, as soon as you have property, assets, and investments, start thinking about making your will and putting a property and finance LPA in place. You should consider a health and welfare LPA from the age of 18 onwards.

We see many clients who have problems dealing with their parents' affairs because their parents don't have LPAs in place. It causes them a lot of stress and anxiety and eats up an enormous amount of time. So these clients often come in to see us earlier for themselves because they don't want their children to have the same problems.

Traditionally, you'd only think about a power of attorney when you get old — but it's a good idea to put one in place much earlier. You never know what's going to happen.

For example, if you were to fall ill or have an accident and go to hospital for several days or weeks, you'd need to be sure someone could look after your affairs. What if your pipes burst and your house flooded? The insurance company would need to get in touch to sort it out straight away, but if everything is in your name only, the insurance company won't speak to anyone else.

With a power of attorney, you could ask your attorneys to speak to whomever they need to on your behalf.

It takes up to six weeks to register your legal documents with the Office of the Public Guardian — and the whole process could take three months before you're able to use your documents. So don't leave it too long.

And if you think you or someone you love is beginning to lose their mental capacity, get the LPAs done as soon as possible. By the time mental capacity is gone, it'll be too late.

You can go to the Office of the Public Guardian website and create your document online, then get it signed and registered yourself — but it's much better to go and see a solicitor, and make sure you get exactly the right document put in place. The OPG doesn't give legal advice and you want to be sure your documents cover everything you need.

A solicitor will look at everything separately and make sure you or your loved one understand the document, understands the powers they're giving and understands the implications of the whole thing.

Why Choose a Solicitor?

You don't have to use a solicitor or any professional to create an LPA, but it's a good idea to do so — particularly if your family situation is complicated, if your affairs are complicated, or if you're on your own.

A specialist solicitor will do far more for you than simply fill in the forms and get them registered.

Before you decide whether or not to use a solicitor, find one that offers a free initial consultation. At Parfitt Cresswell, we offer a free initial consultation to talk about it. We explain the role of attorneys and how your own individual situation may impact your LPA position.

For example, one of our clients had a son who lived with her and was a joint owner of the property. She wanted to appoint him as her attorney — but that would create problems. If mum lost capacity, he'd be unable to make any decisions about the property because legally he can't act for himself and also for her.

Problems like these aren't always obvious, and by talking to a solicitor you can make sure they don't arise for you. If you don't get advice, it'll be too late by the time you lose capacity.

Summary

- A Power of Attorney is a legal document that allows someone to make decisions for you or act on your behalf if you're no longer able or no longer want to make your own decisions. It's very simple, but extremely valuable to you and your family should you lose mental capacity.
- An Ordinary Power of Attorney is valid while you still have mental capacity to make your own decisions, and enables someone you trust to help you with specific financial or property affairs.
- A Lasting Power of Attorney (LPA) for property and finance gives someone you trust the ability to look after your financial affairs when you're no longer able to make decisions yourself or if you no longer want to.
- An LPA for health and welfare similarly allows someone you trust to make health and welfare decisions for you if you lose mental capacity.
- Strongly consider putting LPAs in place, because if something were to happen to you suddenly, you need to know someone can deal with your finances and any health and wellbeing decisions. Without an LPA, everything would grind to a halt. Not even your

spouse can automatically deal with your bank account, pensions, or healthcare decisions without one.

- When you make a property and finance LPA, register it with all your banks, financial institutions, utility companies, and the post office so your attorney can easily deal with anything they need to.
- Consider choosing more than one attorney, just in case something happens to one of them.
- Choose someone you trust. Most people choose close family or a close friend. You can appoint a professional, like a solicitor, if you don't have any family or friends who are suitable.
- You can set up an LPA on your own, by going to the Office of the Public Guardian and downloading the forms and information pack — but it's a good idea to get specialist advice from a solicitor if there are any complications. A solicitor will also help you avoid any common mistakes that often cause problems.
- The Court of Protection makes decisions on financial or welfare matters for those who lack mental capacity and can't make decisions themselves — and who don't have the relevant power of attorney in place. It can take many months to deal with a situation like this, which is why it's so important to put LPAs in place. It's a court of last resort, so if you have all your affairs in order, your family should never need to use it.
- You can apply to the Court of Protection to become a court-appointed deputy — and you can go to the Court to object to an LPA that's already in place.
- The Court of Protection can help you sell jointly owned property if one owner has died and the other doesn't have mental capacity. If you have a good will and suitable LPA in place, you shouldn't need to do this.
- Start thinking about LPAs now. I don't want to sound morbid, but you never know what might happen and

being prepared could save a lot of pain and heartache later on.

In the next chapter, you can find out about the Court of Protection. In the meantime, though, do think carefully about putting LPAs in place if you haven't already done so.

Your Notes

Chapter 9

The Court of Protection

If you don't have valid Power of Attorney documents in place and something happens to the mental capacity of you or your loved one, everything usually falls into the hands of the Court of Protection. It's a last resort because although the Court would be very helpful if you really needed it, it's much better to have everything in place beforehand. It can take a long time and a lot of money to get anything done.

The Court of Protection was created under the Mental Capacity Act 2005 and has jurisdiction over property, financial affairs, and personal welfare.

It's a real court, it's located in High Holborn in London, and hopefully, you'll never have to go there!

The court makes decisions on financial or welfare matters for those who lack mental capacity and can't do it themselves, and who don't have another valid or effective means, such as an appropriate LPA or EPA in place to deal with the issues that need resolving.

It's responsible for a lot, including:

- Deciding if someone has the mental capacity to make a particular decision for themselves.
- Appointing deputies to make ongoing decisions for people who lack mental capacity.
- Giving people permission to make one-off decisions on behalf of someone who lacks mental capacity.
- Handling urgent or emergency applications where a decision must be made on behalf of someone else without delay.
- Making decisions about an LPA or EPA if there are any issues with them, and considering any objections to their registration.
- Considering applications to make statutory wills or gifts.
- Making decisions about when someone can be deprived of their liberty under the Mental Capacity Act.

If your loved one loses mental capacity without appointing an attorney and they can no longer make the appropriate LPAs, you'll have to apply to the Court of Protection for permission to act for them.

For example, say your loved one copes well on their own until they have a fall or a stroke — then they deteriorate. If they're still able to create LPAs, that's great. The people they choose can start acting for them when they need help. But if they lose mental capacity altogether before making the documents, they'll be unable to do so. Someone needs to look after their finances, arrange care, and organise their affairs and this need arises straight away.

It's very difficult to deal with this in an emergency situation because it's generally a very slow process. It's not unknown for cases to take ten months or longer to go through the Court of Protection. This is why it's so important to put powers of attorney in place.

The Court of Protection is like a court of last resort: it's a great safety net, but if you have all your affairs in order and valid LPAs in place, you should never need to use it.

Often you want to be able to manage the loved one's finances generally, and possibly for the long-term, and if that's the case then you'll probably need to apply for deputyship.

How To Become a Court Appointed Deputy

If your loved one loses mental capacity without putting an LPA in place, you can apply to become a court-appointed deputy if you're aged 18 or over. Deputies are usually close relatives or friends of the person who needs help making decisions.

If you want to become a property and finance deputy, you need to have the skills and confidence to make financial decisions for someone else.

The court can appoint one or more deputies for the same person. When there's more than one deputy the court will tell you how to make decisions. It will be either:

- Jointly, which means all the deputies have to agree on the decision together.
- Jointly and severally, which means deputies can make decisions on their own or with other deputies.

Some people, such as solicitors, accountants, or local authority representatives, are paid to act as deputies.

Alternatively, the Court of Protection can appoint a specialist deputy (called a "panel deputy") from a list of approved law firms and charities if no one else is available.

If you do become a deputy, you'll have to take out insurance to protect your loved one and yourself. If you mismanage their funds, the insurance may pay out for them (although this isn't guaranteed).

Financial deputies are rarely given full discretion to manage everything for the incapacitated person freely. They can usually only act within limitations laid out in the court order, such as transactions under a certain value. If they need to do something they still don't have permission for, they must apply to the court again.

The deputy will also usually be told to submit annual accounts.

For health and welfare issues, the court will rarely appoint a deputy on a general basis — the deputy will need to apply to make decisions on an individual basis.

For all these "extra" actions, you'll need to pay more fees to the court. For these reasons, it's generally best to make Lasting Powers of Attorney before losing mental capacity.

One-Off Applications

You might not need full deputyship in some cases and you can ask for permission to make decisions on a one-off basis.

For example, say someone moves into a care home and is perfectly capable of writing a cheque for her fees when she first arrives. If her capacity then deteriorates, she may no longer be able to cope with writing cheques.

If the lady has no expenses other than the care home, you could apply to the Court of Protection for one-off permission to access her bank account and set up a direct debit to the care home so her fees are taken care of.

Selling Jointly Owned Property

The Court of Protection usually has to get involved in property sales when two people own a property jointly but one has died and the other has lost the mental capacity to make decisions and did not make a suitable Power of Attorney document in advance.

Both property owners need to sign, and now one person can't. Perhaps the incapacitated owner doesn't have a Power of Attorney document at all, or perhaps it only appoints the other owner of the property.

Perhaps deputyship has been obtained, but the order didn't give the deputy permission to deal with property.

Someone will probably need to apply to the court for permission to act on the incapacitated person's behalf.

What Forms Do You Need to Complete?

It depends on the exact question you're asking the court to deal with, and the circumstances of each case, but usually to start with you'll need to complete a Court of Protection Application form (COP1). This directs you to other forms.

You'll also need to complete an Assessment of Capacity form (COP3) and pay a fee of £400.

You might have to pay more if the court decides there needs to be a hearing. You may be able to get help to pay the fees. In any case, it's a good idea to get advice from a solicitor, who'll be able to help you get everything in order.

Summary

- The Court of Protection was created under the Mental Capacity Act 2005 and has jurisdiction over property, financial affairs, and personal welfare — it comes into play if you don't have a suitable Power of Attorney document in place.
- You can apply to the Court of Protection for deputyship if a loved one loses mental capacity without appointing an attorney.
- The Court of Protection often gets involved in property sales when two people own a property jointly but one has died and the other has lost the mental capacity to make decisions. It costs £400 to apply (at time of publication) — but may be more, especially if the court decides there needs to be a hearing.
- The Court of Protection can appoint deputies for a person who's lost capacity.
- It's a great safety net, but if you have all your affairs in order and good LPAs in place, you and your family should never need to use the Court of Protection.

In the next chapter, we'll look at what to do if you're thinking of downsizing and moving home.

Your Notes

Chapter 10

Thinking About Downsizing

Imagine taking the holiday of a lifetime! Six weeks travelling Australia and New Zealand.

It's all planned out: the flights, the hotels, the cities, and the sights. And there are a few days free for relaxing... or seeing something you didn't know was there.

Insurance is sorted — after all, when you're that far from home, you want to know you're covered.

You know exactly where you need to be, when, and how to get there. And you know what to do if something should go wrong.

This is one holiday, which you've been planning for months, if not years. You know exactly where to start and where you're going...

But what about the next stage of your life?

It's funny: we spend so much time planning for children, planning an education, planning a career, planning weddings and parties, planning retirement, and planning holidays — but when it comes to old age and the end of life, we pull the covers over our heads and pretend it's not happening.

We tuck it away in the backs of our minds, vowing to cross that bridge when we come to it.

The problem is, that bridge is going to get shakier and shakier as we get older, and this problem will become more and more difficult to deal with.

The idea of getting older, creakier, less capable, and more dependent isn't particularly pleasant. Nobody really wants to face it.

Our families don't want to face it, either.

Mum and dad, for most of us, represent strength. They've always taken care of us, they seem to have all the answers, and they get things done.

So when parents start to get older and need a little more help, it's scary — for them and for us. Age creeps up on us gradually.

Then, suddenly, it's too late. We haven't planned for a change in lifestyle, so change is thrust upon us — and it's not always what we'd want.

Because nobody really wants to think about this stage of life, we don't do anything to plan for it. And that creates a huge gap filled with painful problems.

Instead of a life of choice and the leisure to choose what happens next, older people struggle through a distressed transition.

Wouldn't you rather grow older and change your lifestyle on your terms?

If you don't make plans to move into a smaller home, or into sheltered accommodation, it will happen when it has to happen — when you have no more options.

It will happen when you simply can't stay where you are anymore.

And what does happen might not be what you'd choose.

There are many reasons why you might have to move out of your family home. Some people find they can no longer get upstairs or cope with the size of the house. Others find money is much tighter than it used to be, and a bigger house is too expensive to run.

Some spend years relying on friends and neighbours who are suddenly no longer able to help.

There are many, many circumstances that can force you out of your home and into a smaller place, or into sheltered accommodation.

And when you're forced out of your home, you're left with little choice. You have to deal with everything in a rush, under great pressure — and you may not end up where you would have liked to if you'd had time to plan.

But if you treat growing older as you'd treat the holiday of a lifetime, you can make a plan that suits you and your family.

You can avoid being pushed around by circumstances.

You can avoid the extreme stress that comes with having to make big decisions under pressure.

And you can turn the whole process of downsizing, decluttering, and moving on into a pleasant adventure.

"We should have done this years ago…"

One of the most common phrases we hear from older people when it comes to downsizing, is, "We should have done this years ago!"

Getting older and moving out of the family home isn't something most of us think about until the situation becomes urgent.

Downsizing seems like a huge undertaking, and it's one we put off for as long as possible — but once you've made the transition, you'll be glad you did.

So start planning as early as possible — even as early as when you start thinking about retirement. That might seem premature, but you don't know how your health will be in the future. You don't know what will happen to your family situation or your finances.

Consider what stage you're at as soon as possible.

You might want to downsize a little when you first retire — but perhaps won't be ready for a small one-bedroomed apartment. And you certainly won't be ready for sheltered accommodation.

Planning for the future is all about thinking ahead and being open to the idea of things changing. You might be moving now, into a smaller place… but will it still be suitable in 10 years?

Think beyond what you need now and consider how suitable your home and environment will be when you start to get older and less capable. Will you really want to move and do the transition again?

You might — and if so, that's fine.

But giving it some proper thought now means you'll be prepared for anything.

Stress, Anxiety, and Overwhelm

The biggest sources of stress and anxiety facing most older people when they have to move home are:

1. The sheer volume of stuff we own.
2. Having to make big decisions under pressure.
3. The emotional attachment we have to our stuff.

How do you get from a large family home filled with things you've gathered over decades to a small apartment with little or no storage?

Nobody wants to face dealing with mountains of stuff, so people ignore it for as long as they can.

It's understandable because downsizing feels like climbing Everest — it's a huge and insurmountable task, and you have no idea where to start.

So you don't start at all.

Dealing with a complicated project like moving house gets harder as you get older. There's a lot to think about — especially as you're carrying more worries around in your head. You may also be facing health concerns for yourself or your spouse. And you may be concerned about how this change will affect your family.

It may be years since you last had to deal with moving home: the buying and selling, estate agents and their overblown promises, solicitors and their legalese, the endless paperwork...

There's no getting around it: downsizing, like climbing Everest, is a big project. But here's the thing: nobody climbs Everest in one go.

They tackle it one step at a time.

You can tackle downsizing and decluttering in the same way.

You don't have to do it all at once and you don't have to do it alone.

Make a plan. Get support.

Start with the end in mind, as you would with a holiday: what's your destination? Where do you want to go? How do you want your lifestyle to be?

Sit down and talk it through with someone you trust. That might be a family member... although sometimes, with the best of intentions, family can be more of a hindrance than a help. It might be a friend.

Or you could get professional help if you need to.

But start by talking it through and making a plan.

Making A Plan

Downsizing simply means reducing the amount of stuff you own and deciding what you want to take with you.

What do you feel you need at your particular stage of life?

Chances are, you'll have to get rid of a lot of stuff — and this will take time to organise. The last thing you want to do is make hasty decisions you might regret later, so give yourself at least three months to thin out your belongings.

Start by going around your home, room by room, and making a list of items you can't live without. Anything that doesn't make this list is potentially expendable.

It can be daunting to think about getting rid of things with

131

emotional attachments, so many people find it helpful to start with practicalities.

For example, if you're moving to a flat without a private garden you probably won't need a lawn mower or a ladder.

If you're moving from a three-bedroom property to a one-bedroom place, you can dispose of the extra beds, mattresses, and sheets. Plus, you can get rid of the furniture that goes in those rooms.

Go through your bedrooms, loft, garage, and kitchen. These are all rooms with clutter you can live without. There's something about mugs... most homes have a lot of them, collected over the years — but how many do you really need? And it's the same with glasses. I don't know about you, but I have more than I'll ever need in one go!

Do you have tools you've rarely — or never — used? Are there spare TVs, a neglected exercise bike, and other valuable but little-used items lurking in the corners of your rooms?

When you start the process of decluttering, ask yourself the following questions to help you decide what to keep and what to pass on:

- When was the last time I used this?
- If I do use it, how often do I use it, and why? What purpose does it serve?
- Do I own something else that does the same thing?
- Is this item something I love? Does it have sentimental value that can't be replaced?
- Can I get by without it or will I have to replace it if I get rid of it?
- Is it in good condition? Will it last for a long time?
- Does it need repair, and if so, how much will it cost? Is it worth repairing?
- Do I know someone else who would benefit a lot more from this thing?
- Will I need it in this new life I'm moving to?

Decluttering can be an emotionally fraught process, which

is why many people resist it. But leaving it until the last minute can be traumatic and panicked, and often results in hasty decisions.

Leaving plenty of time for decluttering and downsizing, though, can turn the whole process into a lovely experience…

A Life Story In Dresses

Instead of looking at decluttering and downsizing as a chore to get out of the way, you could turn it into a fun experience.

Ask someone to come and help — and while you're making decisions and going through your stuff, take the opportunity to tell stories, relive experiences, and share your life.

Eyes and faces light up as long-forgotten photographs or clothes or treasured possessions are found and remembered.

One lady told us her life story in dresses!

Going through her wardrobe, she pulled out one dress after another, all from when she was young.

With each dress came a story: amazing, glamorous events and parties she'd attended… Interesting people she'd met… Fascinating places and countries she'd visited…

And as she told the stories, she transported herself — and us — back in time. By being able to share those stories, she could let them go — and letting go of her beautiful dresses became much, much easier.

Being able to share special moments can be very therapeutic. It's not often in our busy lives that we get the chance to reminisce — and that's a shame because most people have lived good and interesting lives and have lots of great stories to tell.

We've had lots of laughs with our clients over the years: funny stories surface about how things used to be done — all sparked by finding some old-fashioned gadget in the back of a kitchen cupboard.

When you turn a chore into a pleasant experience, people who are resistant to decluttering start to enjoy it. They get into their stride and are able to make decisions more quickly, without feeling backed into a corner or under pressure from family and friends.

If you can find a way to manage this process that works for you, you'll find it much easier and much more enjoyable.

And if you can find someone you trust to help you, all the better.

Family and Friends

When it comes to asking for help, though, remember: families can sometimes make things more difficult, despite having the best intentions to help.

It's easy to forget that although this transition to a new stage of life is personal to a parent or grandparent, it affects the whole family — and often friends, too.

The whole process of decluttering and downsizing can throw up lots of issues you may not even be aware of. Personal grievances and old wounds can bubble up from childhood, and all kinds of issues can get in the way of building productive and close relationships.

If you're preparing to declutter and downsize, take the time to explain how you're feeling and why to your family. If you sense they're getting impatient, sit them down and explain. Remember what it was like to be young, and busy, and distracted — they don't mean to dismiss your feelings, they just don't realise what they are.

And of course, if you have a parent or grandparent who's downsizing, this section will help you avoid any misunderstandings — and reduce the likelihood of any family rows. Understanding why someone may be resistant to decluttering, and grasping how emotional it is, can help enormously.

One of the biggest problems comes when grown-up children make big general promises to help — with every intention of keeping them — but then fail to follow through. We all have busy lives, and our lives can get in the way.

So instead of making a vague promise to come and help get the whole thing done sometime before moving day, instead be specific. Suggest coming to help with one particular thing on a specific date.

That way, everyone knows where they stand.

We all feel awkward asking, "When are you coming?" We feel like we're nagging. And older people especially don't want to feel like they're being a bother.

If you put a firm date in the diary to help with something specific, it's much easier to deliver on your promise.

Remember to only promise what you can actually deliver, too. It's easy to feel guilty about a parent or grandparent's change of circumstances, and that can lead us to overcompensate by making promises we'll struggle to fulfil.

Don't feel guilty if your busy life means you can't help. It's better your parents know this — they'll be grateful for your honesty, which will allow them to make other arrangements.

By planning for downsizing early, and getting the process started a few months in advance, you'll have plenty of time to get everything done without rushing.

There'll be lots of opportunities for everyone to help out.

Doing things at the last minute can make things much more complicated — logistically and personally.

When moving is rushed, it's very common for younger people to get frustrated at their parents' slower speed and inability to make decisions.

When you have time to go through possessions with care, you're much less likely to dismiss important stuff and upset your family.

And you're much less likely to feel pressured into doing something you don't want to do.

If you really do struggle to make progress and hit an impasse as a family, mediators can help enormously. They're neutral, and they'll help everyone see the others' point of view — and get the task done calmly and with care.

Getting Professional Help

I hope this chapter has helped you see moving house, downsizing, and decluttering doesn't have to be a nightmare.

But even with careful planning, it's still a big project — and there's still a lot to think about.

Perhaps your family live too far away to help as much as they'd like.

Or maybe you don't feel physically up to the task of moving.

Did you know you can get professional help from businesses dedicated to later life planning? Although this type of service has been around for a while in America, it's relatively new to the UK.

At Parfitt Cresswell, we work closely with a number of professionals who support our clients and help them plan for later life. Felicity Bunt at Senior Services is one of them. I asked her to explain what help is available for older people.

She told me this story about her client, Mrs G.

Mrs G contacted Senior Services when she needed help to move from her four-bedroom home with a large garden to a new two-bedroom apartment in a retirement community 50 miles away. Her husband had died several years earlier and she was finally ready to move on and find a home that better suited her needs and lifestyle. With no family, Mrs G also wanted to make sure she'd have the support and care she might need in years to come.

Felicity met Mrs G and talked through the move so she could understand her hopes and concerns before agreeing on a support plan. The first step was to begin decluttering. Over several weeks, Felicity and her team guided Mrs G to make difficult decisions about what to take with her. Mrs G discovered that, despite her hesitation to let go of many of her belongings, she enjoyed remembering and sharing special moments in her life as cupboards, wardrobes and drawers gradually gave up their contents for inspection.

Senior Services arranged for charities, house clearance

companies, and auctioneers to donate, sell or dispose of any possessions Mrs G no longer wanted.

Then, having visited and measured up the new apartment, Senior Services created a floor-plan using the furniture Mrs G wanted to take, to make sure it would all fit and to make sure the room layouts would be uncluttered and safe. They arranged for a new phone line to be installed, managed the notification to utilities, and researched the best tariffs for her new address. They also helped to notify all Mrs G's contacts about her new address.

Senior Services organised and managed the whole move, acting as a single point of contact for the removals company, estate agent, retirement community, and other third parties. They also made sure Mrs G paced herself on moving day, taking regular breaks and refreshments, so she didn't exhaust herself.

Once the furniture and boxes were unloaded into the apartment, Senior Services got busy unpacking and setting up Mrs G's new home. They prepared the kitchen, stocked the fridge, made the bed, put clothes away, unwrapped china, glassware and ornaments, put books on bookshelves and took away all packaging materials.

Throughout the whole process, Mrs G found one of the greatest benefits came from the ongoing personal support of a trusted professional. She had access to guidance on how best to respond to a wide range of issues relating to the sale and purchase of her homes. There was always someone available to listen to her concerns, providing reassurance, understanding and focus.

Mrs G continues to work with Senior Services' Trusted Guardian service for ongoing home management support. It's tailored to her needs and the Trusted Guardian helps with paying bills, reviewing and renewing policies and agreements, filing, making appointments, advocating on her behalf, and offers guidance and support on personal matters.

Not everyone needs or wants a professional to be involved

— but for those whose families live far away or are too busy, or who don't have any family at all, they can be a real treasure.

Later life planning services help older people with all aspects of moving home, downsizing, moving from hospitals to care homes — or wherever they go next.

Professionals are there to help with whatever needs to be done to move you from A to B — and they'll help you and your family deal with property and other practical aspects of moving home. An organisation like Senior Services can work with you to:

- Help you assess your home options, including "ageing in place".
- Advise on moving, whether locally or across country.
- Create a moving plan that meets your individual needs.
- Organise and manage all aspects of the move, liaising with you and your family.
- Declutter for auction, charity and family.
- Stage your home so it looks its best for prospective buyers.
- Source removal companies.
- Arrange change of address notification for utilities and services.
- Liaise with estate agent and other third parties.
- Oversee the packing and unpacking.
- Arrange furniture as per your bespoke floor-plan.
- Make beds, prepare bathroom and kitchen.
- Arrange cleaning, property repairs, waste removal and recycling, decorating.
- Co-ordinate connection to gas, electricity, water, telephone, TV, IT and other suppliers.
- Arrange care for pets if required.
- Ensure the vacated property is empty, clean and secure.
- Coaching and counselling for older people and families to help you and them cope with the change that comes with ageing, retirement, and later life transitions.

People who work with professionals often find the greatest value comes not just from the practical side of things, but from the personal support throughout. You have access to project managers who'll hold your hand throughout and help you cope with the unexpected when it arises.

With a little extra help and support, a big project like moving home and changing circumstances becomes very manageable.

Preparing for later life is very important if you wish to remain independent and in control for as long as possible, however, it does require some thought and planning.

By considering your housing options and other factors now, you will be better placed to enjoy your retirement and later years.

If you decide to engage a business like Senior Services, make sure it's a member of the National Association of Senior Move Managers (NASMM). Based in the USA, NASMM is the leading international membership organisation for the senior move management industry.

Full members must meet strict vetting requirements before approval, and must have business liability insurance. They must have completed specific training, and provide letters of recommendation from former clients.

Members abide by the NASMM Code of Ethics, which means they're committed to safety and committed to continuing professional development.

Attendance at meetings, conferences, and training courses as well as sharing experiences and learning from each other, ensures they stay up to date with the latest issues. All members should also have had criminal record checks.

Check they work to a code of ethics, and ask for references.

To find out more in a confidential conversation, contact:

Felicity Bunt, Director

Tel: 07939 042 805

E: info@seniorservicesmanagement.co.uk

W: www.seniorservicesmanagement.co.uk

Summary

- We spend more time planning our holidays than we do planning what will happen when we get old and reach the end of our lives — yet planning for old age is probably one of the most important things we can do.

- By planning in advance, you can avoid being pushed around by circumstances, you can avoid the extreme stress that comes from making decisions in crisis, and you can turn the whole process of downsizing into a pleasure rather than a chore.

- The biggest sources of stress and anxiety facing most older people when they have to move are the sheer volume of stuff, having to make big decisions under pressure, and emotional attachments to possessions.

- Start by making a plan: don't just dive in and try to deal with it all at once, spend plenty of time going through what you own and make calm decisions.

- Turn your clear-out into a trip down memory lane, and ask for help from someone who'll enjoy hearing your stories.

- Talk to your family in plenty of time, and when they offer to help put firm dates and tasks in place — avoid vague promises and be specific about what you can all do.

- Consider bringing in professional help, especially if you don't have family who can help you — a caring professional will help you make difficult decisions, deal with all the logistics, and be there when you need a little extra support.

In Chapter 11, you'll discover how to go about finding and choosing a suitable care home.

Your Notes

Chapter 11

Finding and Choosing a Care Home

There are two huge problems with care homes in the UK.

Firstly, there's simply not enough useful information easily available.

And secondly, we have a terribly skewed impression of what care homes are like, thanks to many negative stories in the media.

I'm hoping this chapter will change your view of care and encourage you to think about your options early.

You'll find out what type of care is available, when to start planning and thinking about it, and how to choose a suitable place.

For most people, going into care happens randomly, decisions are made back to front and at the last minute — and that's absolutely the worst thing that can happen.

Decisions are made in crisis without any planning at all. Why? Because we don't like talking about getting older and dying. We don't even like to think about it.

This is a relatively new phenomenon. Even just 100 years ago, people were quite open about death because it happened at home, in the front room. These days, it's locked away in care homes and sterilised in hospitals. It's hidden, denied, and ignored.

And it shouldn't be.

This way of thinking about things and doing things is painful. It's damaging. And it leads to older people languishing on their own, struggling for too long — then going to unsuitable or undesirable care homes.

Before we start on the practicalities of choosing care homes, though, I want to tell you about Tony.

Tony was a lifelong bachelor with no children. He was mentally fit and well, but at 78 years old, his body was letting him down. He was hunched over, and could no longer get down the step of his front or back door.

He'd been housebound for two years, relying on meals on wheels and eating out of a foil tray. The meal delivery person was the only person he spoke to each day.

In fact, his life had become terribly sad: he had cereal for breakfast, Meals on Wheels for lunch, and a cup of soup for dinner every day.

His neighbour was helpful and shopped for him once a fortnight, but he couldn't really look after himself.

All his friends had died, he couldn't do anything, and spent his whole life in a few downstairs rooms, because he couldn't get upstairs to sleep or bathe. He was isolated.

It wasn't until he fell out of bed and had to call an ambulance that he decided enough was enough. That was his trigger point.

He was put in touch with Debbie, a professional who matches people with care homes.

She started researching care homes in the south of England. She couldn't take him with her on daily visits because he was too immobile, but she took photographs, made notes, and sat with him over a cup of tea and cake to go through his options.

They decided to look at a place on the coast, so Debbie took him there for lunch and showed him around.

Lunch was served on linen table clothes, with silver service, china, cutlery, and napkins. There was a glass of wine and a choice of three meals with starter and dessert.

Other residents came and introduced themselves, and Tony spoke to more people in that one day than he had in a year.

Four weeks later, he moved in.

The apartment he chose had a lounge with a balcony and sea view, a kitchenette so he could store a bottle of wine and make a cup of tea, a bedroom, and an en-suite bathroom. He also had 24-hour support from carers.

When Debbie went back to visit, she asked him how he was getting on.

"I"m fluffy!" he said. "I've washed my hair for the first time in two years!"

He had new dentures, his toenails and fingernails were looked after, and he had new — larger — trousers (a result of finally eating well). He was a new man.

But perhaps best of all, he's happy. He's living his life now, not simply existing. He used to claim he liked his own company... but now he chairs the residents' meeting and meets four ladies every day for lunch.

The first part of Tony's story — his two years of being housebound and existing on Meals on Wheels — isn't unusual. The lack of planning and forward thinking is common. The decision made in crisis, after a fall, is standard for older people in the UK.

For some, that's it. That's what later living is until they get seriously ill and go for a final stay in the hospital.

But for others, like Tony, there's a whole new lease of life waiting in some wonderful accommodation.

And the best way to make sure of a wonderful later life is to find out as much as you can about your options and make clear plans.

Staying Independent

Many people are very resistant to leaving their family home and going into care or sheltered accommodation.

That's understandable because your home is where your heart lies. It's full of memories. And the constant negative portrayals of the care industry in the media is enough to put anyone off.

But one of the most common things I hear people say after they've made the move is: "We should have done this years ago."

Everyone wants to stay independent for as long as possible, but many people stay independent for too long. They find it more and more difficult to get out and see people, so they become isolated. With no stimulation and no social contact, there's no incentive to eat properly, to cook, to talk to people — and they deteriorate fast.

They begin to realise it'd be a good idea to get some help, but moving into care is a huge decision — and now they're struggling to cope alone, it's even more difficult to decide.

If people thought about this earlier, it would be much easier. Going to coffee mornings at local care homes, and visiting residents would help to remove the fear of the unknown — and it would help to dispel myths about care home horror stories.

People generally don't start thinking about care homes until a loved one becomes ill and the carer needs some respite. Very many people who go in for respite care tend to stay permanently because they realise how much of a better quality of life they'll have.

Another common reason is crisis: someone finds themselves in trouble, often after a fall, and goes into hospital. The hospital fixes that problem, but the person often deteriorates in hospital and the hospital won't let them go home alone.

A care home is needed, and the typical mad panic ensues to find somewhere suitable.

And then there's the odd rare individual who makes the decision themselves. On occasion, someone will decide they're getting less capable and will plan to move into care in a few months. They do research — or get someone to research on their behalf — and have it all planned out. This is the ideal situation because they stay in control.

It's really unfortunate that almost all families leave this important, emotional, expensive, and life-changing decision until the last minute, making choices under enormous stress and in a very short space of time.

Leaving it until it's an emergency often only leaves families with a week to find somewhere suitable — and that's a tall order even for professionals. There's no way to make a good decision when you have work and family to think about too.

It makes so much sense to start thinking about this early, and it's much easier to do so if you focus on the many positive aspects of going into care. For the most part, it's nothing at all like the negative media coverage.

Care homes can be hugely supportive of someone who's lonely because they'll be surrounded by like-minded people. They'll never be bored because most care homes have a lot going on: communal meals, entertainment, games, and organised trips. And for those with dementia, they get the proper care they need.

The Three Main Types of Care Home

You may have heard the term "assisted living" or "supported living". These terms cover a wide variety of living spaces, but it's generally accommodation with staff onsite between 9 am and 5 pm. They're not true residential care homes, but they do offer a little more support and peace of mind.

These places range from one-room bedsits to pretty luxurious three-bedroomed apartments. You're limited only by price, and you tend to rent such places by the week (as with care homes).

Then there are retirement villages. These are homes you buy rather than rent, usually, and they're designed with older people in mind. They can be great places because they often have lots of facilities: a swimming pool, library, restaurant, bistro — even a farm, a church, and a theatre in some cases.

Some are huge — up to 100 acres, with more than 350 apartments including care homes. These are a great option for those thinking ahead, who aren't ready for residential care, but who do want to live in a protected environment with like-minded people and domiciliary care on hand.

As for care homes, there are three fundamental types. They're residential — you live there — and you can go in for respite care or you can stay there permanently.

Residential care homes provide personal support and care. You can get help with washing, dressing, going to bed, eating, and even mobility. It's for people who need a little extra help and support, but don't need a nurse.

Nursing care includes all the above, but with a registered nurse on the premises 24 hours a day, seven days a week.

There's a little ambiguity with residential care homes that call in doctors and nurses for support, but it really depends on the care home and the individual resident.

If you have extensive mobility problems, and particularly if you need two people to help you move or you need a hoist, you'd probably need to choose a nursing home whether you need a nurse or not. Most residential care homes generally don't have the staff, skills, or equipment to provide that level of support.

Because of the blurred lines between residential and nursing care, it's very important to discuss with each care home you consider exactly what level of care and mobility support they can offer.

It's also why planning and forward thinking is so important. You can't always tell what's going to happen in future, but you can make an educated guess. Detailed discussions with the care home, the individual, and doctors can help you find the right accommodation without having to worry about moving somewhere else a few months down the line.

The final category is dementia care. People with dementia may need residential care or nursing care, or a combination — but it's important to check whether or not your chosen care home can cope with differing levels of dementia.

Research from the Alzheimer's Society found at least two-thirds of people in residential care homes have some form of dementia. Dementia ranges from mild forgetfulness to very challenging behaviour — and those with severe dementia can be very difficult to place in care homes.

If you or a loved one has dementia, it's very important to understand how it's likely to progress so you can choose a care home that's best able to cope and provide support.

When someone develops dementia, it can be very difficult if they're in a retirement village or assisted living accommodation because they will have to move to a specialist care setting.

The ideal pathway follows this pattern: private home to a retirement village or assisted living, to a final care home.

Pricing and the level of care you can expect varies enormously.

Right at the bottom are Local Authority-funded care homes. In the south of England, Local Authority-funded care homes can cost as little as £450 a week. The most expensive privately funded care homes can cost as much as £2,000 a week.

If you can possibly avoid it, you do not want to go into a Local Authority home. Funding is extremely limited and while they do their best, it's not what most of us would choose.

This is why planning your later life finances carefully is so very important.

The level of care you get varies hugely, too, and it's not necessarily reflected in the price you pay.

Truly good care is sincere, kind, and supportive. You want to know that when you or your loved one wake up at 3 am needing help to go to the loo, the person who helps is kind and happy to be there.

It doesn't matter how luxurious the surroundings are if the staff aren't loving and caring. You want a friendly, personal service — it's the little things that make the difference.

The big things are usually fine because all care homes have to comply with the Care Quality Commission (CQC) rules. Over and above that, the individual staff make or break a care home.

Don't assume that just because a care home is expensive, it'll be the best option. Our care home experts have eaten in many care homes and have been horrified at the low quality of food in some very expensive places.

Conversely, they've visited tiny care homes that could do with a new coat of paint and a bit of TLC — but the staff have been friendly and welcoming, and the food has been superb.

Whether you need residential care, nursing care, or dementia care, it's vital to do your research. But how do you make a final decision?

The Four Key Care Home Questions

Before you start looking for a care home, there are four key questions you need to ask yourself.

1. Where does the care home need to be located?

A fundamental mistake many families make is choosing a care home that's too far away from where the main visitor lives. For example, we know of a family whose daughter lives in Devon and the son lives in London, so they chose a care home for their mother that was halfway between them.

This was a big mistake because it took both children four hours to get to mum, and they only visited rarely.

This is a classic mistake that springs from the best intentions to be fair.

In most families with more than one grown-up child, though, one of the children is the main visitor. So be brutally honest and decide who will visit most often — and choose a care home nearest to that person.

You'll also find price can significantly influence the location, so bear that in mind when you're looking.

Another common mistake is thinking you need to choose a care home in a particular location because the parent has always lived there. But unless the person has lots of family and friends in the area, they probably won't go out much.

The deciding factor should be how easy it is for family and friends to visit, not whether it's in an area they've always lived.

2. What type of care do you need?

It's very important to understand whether you'll need residential care or nursing care. You may not know for sure what will happen in the future, but you do need some understanding — even if only to exclude residential care.

If you know you'll need a nurse, don't look at residential homes.

If you know you or your loved one will have significant mobility problems, don't look at standard residential care.

If you're concerned about dementia, only look at homes that work with dementia residents — and consider the level of dementia and what the likely progression will be.

When you identify a short-list in the location you want with the type of care you want, give them a call to discuss in detail. Make sure they can meet your needs before you go and see them.

3. The price.

It is absolutely vital you understand what you can afford. Please read the chapter on later living finances carefully, because there's lots of advice and information about planning for your later years and making sure you have plenty of money not just for your basic care, but for enjoying your life too.

You should also consider talking to a SOLLA (Society of Later Life Advisors) financial advisor about care funding. SOLLA is a not-for-profit organisation that gives care fees advice.

Price affects many things, but it's not the most important

thing to determine the quality of care. You may find two care homes that offer the same level of care at very different prices.

Make sure you understand your budget first before you go to see any care homes. It's quite common for people to visit care homes, fall in love with them, then find out they can't afford it.

It's also very important to understand your finances so you can make sure you can afford to stay there long term. You may well be able to afford somewhere for a couple of years — only to run out of money and have to move on, which can be very stressful and unsettling.

Finance has to be a key criterion so you can choose the right care home from the start. You don't want to have to move for any reason.

4. Is the care home you want available?

Many people mistakenly think they can book a room at a care home in advance — but you can't, for the most part. When you find the right place, you need to be able to move within a couple of weeks. So if you do your research, and plan in advance, you'll be able to move before it becomes urgent, rather than scramble in a panic at the last minute during a crisis.

Planning ahead enables you to make important decisions when you're less stressed. You'll be more informed, more in control, and the care home you choose will likely be more appropriate for what you want and need.

Availability of rooms in care homes is last minute, but all your research should come very early on. That way, you can move when your chosen accommodation becomes available.

These are the four most important criteria to consider when choosing your care home, but there are other things to consider, too.

When you've worked through those four questions and come up with a shortlist, choose three you like the look of and visit them all.

Go in, have lunch, and look around. Visit at different times of the day. Talk to residents if you can, and find out what they think of the place.

Talk to staff, too, and find out how many people work at night and at weekends, and what the staffing ratios are. How many agency staff do they have? If they have lots of agency staff, that can be a sign they're struggling to keep staff, which will affect the level of care you receive.

Check the CQC report, too. It's a blunt instrument, and it may be out of date, but check it anyway because it will tell you whether or not the care homes you've chosen to look at are meeting minimum standards.

Finally, just spend some time there. Consider: will I or my loved one fit in and make friends? Does it feel right?

Consider what type of home your loved one will feel most comfortable in. For example, would a communal bathroom be acceptable, or must it be a private en-suite?

Would you or your loved ones cope with a purpose-built modern care home, or would you be more comfortable in a conversion?

Purpose-built homes will be large, often with more than 80 bedrooms and separated into sections. They can feel bigger, more corporate, and can seem intimidating for people used to small places or villages.

A smaller converted home with more old-fashioned furniture and decor may be more comfortable and familiar for older folks from a different generation.

Consider, too, if you're a couple or you're looking for a care home for a couple. Men's life expectancy is catching up with women's now, so there will be more and more couples who don't want to be separated. It's a more difficult search, but larger rooms do exist in older homes and in purpose-built complexes.

Most care homes have a single room with a single bed, but some have self-contained suites with twin beds, a lounge, a bathroom, and a kitchenette.

Some suites even have two bedrooms.

Care providers are beginning to realise people who are

downsizing don't necessarily want to move into a tiny, one-room place. And as our population ages, we'll get more and more choice over where we want to spend our later years.

The Practicalities of Moving

Chapter 10 told you everything you need to know about downsizing and decluttering, but there are a few things specific to care homes you might want to consider.

Take as many personal items as you can, so the environment looks as familiar and comfortable as possible.

For example, if you or your loved one has a favourite chair, take it — but also take the side table and all the bits and pieces that go along with the chair. Do the same with the bedside table.

Take favourite photographs too, especially if they have dementia. Looking through photo albums helps people to remember what they need to know.

Keep in mind the size of the room, too — you want plenty of familiar items, but not so many you can barely move!

But for nursing care at the end of life, there may be less need for so many personal items.

Bear in mind that care homes usually want clothes labelled so they don't get lost during the laundry service.

As for moving in, some care homes can collect you and your belongings. Sometimes the family will drive you in and arrange for belongings to come along.

But often, the person will be going straight from the hospital to their new home, so the family will need to arrange to move furniture and personal items.

It's really useful to nominate one person who's the sole point of contact and who manages everything. When someone goes into a care home, you'll have to deal with several different organisations.

It's better if the point of contact can be a daughter or son, or another family member, rather than a spouse. The spouse will be providing emotional support and often dealing with tremendous guilt, too, if they're not moving into a care home together. If you're thinking about helping mum or dad to move into a care home, remember this will be a very difficult and emotional time, and you'll need to be patient and understanding.

When someone's lived with their partner for such a long time — maybe 70 years — they often feel terribly guilty about "passing them on".

The nominated person should also make sure they sort out and take as much paperwork as possible, so it all stays organised and together.

And when you're organising visits, try to space them out to allow mum or dad to get settled in. Have everyone visit at different times of the month, rather than all turning up on one day.

You're Not Alone

All this might seem very overwhelming, and it can be.

Looking for information about care homes can feel a little like arriving at a giant railway station like Charing Cross. There are thousands of people going in all directions, announcements over the tannoys, signage everywhere, noise and bustle.

It's terribly confusing.

But at the train station, everyone ends up in more-or-less the right place, because there's a central ticket office and plenty of signage to tell you what to do and where to go.

When it comes to care homes, though, it's like arriving at Charing Cross station in an alternative universe where everyone's milling around, there are no directions, no ticket office, and no useful information.

Everyone involved in later living has to work together to provide that information, but at the moment nobody is talking to each other.

What usually happens when someone's looking for a care home is they'll Google "care homes Kent" and be bombarded with far too much useless information. They'll often be in crisis, needing to find somewhere at very short notice.

So they'll pick a few care homes at random from the list that pops up, and go and visit. The care homes will show them around, then ask you the important questions.

But, as you now realise, this is the wrong way around. With a little planning and forward thinking, you can choose a care home that's right for you and make sure you do it as effectively and efficiently as possible.

Of course, you don't have to take all this on alone. You may be surprised to learn there are professional organisations to help you deal with all of this. Getting help is a great idea if, like most people, you're juggling full-time work and a family while you're trying to look after mum or dad.

Ultimately, professional organisations are there to support families, individuals, and care professionals to make an informed choice about the type of care home someone will live in.

The vast majority of people have no idea what to do — or even where to start — when it comes to finding later life care.

You might be worried a service like this is very expensive — but actually, it can save you a lot of money, time, and stress.

We work with Debbie Harris, from Chosen With Care, and she gave us a great example of how professionals can help.

"Our service costs £65 per hour, and it takes an average of 10 hours to find suitable accommodation for our clients. That may sound expensive but consider this: one client had looked at around 70 different care homes and still hadn't been able to find one for his mother. He'd taken three weeks off work and was on the verge of losing his job because of it.

He was at the end of his tether and getting desperate when he came to us.

We realised he hadn't considered the four key criteria because he had no idea where to start and no time to do any proper research. Like most people, he was in a crisis situation.

He'd gone into panic mode.

We found the right care home in just four days — and it wasn't one he'd already looked at.

Professional fees are extremely low in comparison to the value clients get — not just in money spent searching, but in time and stress.

We don't just find the care home, though — we also negotiate the care home price for the client. We check availability, because if they have lots of beds available they may reduce the price. Then we pass this saving onto the client. Crucially, we do not take a referral fee from the care home — we work for the family and we become surrogate daughters for the time it takes us to find the very best care home for mum or dad.

We can put you in touch with specialist later living financial advisors and solicitors, too."

Debbie's key piece of advice is this:

"If you're able to do so, think ahead. Get those four key criteria clear in your mind, and think about the future, not just the next six months.

Visit the care homes at different times and get involved. Talk to the staff and work with them to find the best option for you.

And before you do anything else, call the free care home advice line.

We'll talk you through what you need to do to find the very best and most suitable residential, nursing, dementia, or respite care for your loved one.

Call 01892 300 530 or email advice@chosenwithcare.co.uk and we'll talk you through everything you need to think about and do.

If you do decide to work with a professional organisation, check they're totally independent. They shouldn't work for any care homes or take referral fees from any care provider. Their sole objective should be to provide independent and impartial advice to families about how to make an informed decision about care."

Summary

- For most people, going into care happens randomly and in crisis — but with a little forward planning it doesn't have to be that way. Instead of sweeping it under the mat, start thinking about your later years now, so you can make sure they're enjoyable.
- Care homes have had a lot of negative attention in the media, and you do have to choose carefully — but there are a lot of great places out there. They provide daily living support, social contact, and encourage people to stay mentally and physically active for longer.
- The three main types of care home are residential homes providing personal support and care, nursing homes with a registered nurse on-site 24/7, and dementia care, which provides specialist care for those with dementia.
- When you're choosing a care home, look beyond the surroundings and talk to the staff and residents. Is everyone happy there?
- Before you start looking, ask the four key questions: location, type of care you need, price, and availability.
- Choosing a care home is a big task and it takes a lot of time and energy. Consider asking a professional to help you out. They can save you an enormous amount of time and even negotiate on care fees and help you move in.

Hopefully, though, it'll be some time before you need to move into a care home. In the meantime, what do you think you'll do with your retirement? Chapter 12 will give you some ideas.

Your Notes

Chapter 12

What Will You Do When You Retire?

Have you thought about how you'll spend your time when you retire? What will you do all day?

It's easy to say you'll spend more time with the family, play golf, read more books, join classes and learn something new, travel to all the destinations on your bucket list, learn a new language... our lists are always endless.

But will you actually do any of those things?

What will you really do — and will it bring you fulfilment?

For many people, retirement conjures up thoughts of leisurely days relaxing, with more time to spend with your grandchildren. For others, retirement takes them to the golf course or spending more time enjoying hobbies. For some, it's taking a holiday whenever you want and wherever the fancy takes you.

But for many, the reality of being 55-plus is retirement may come sooner than you expect in the form of a job loss — with little chance of finding other employment.

Some people reach retirement age and find the loss of income prevents them from doing many of the activities they'd like to do. Their financial position simply won't support it.

Then there's the fortunate third category who reach retirement with a reasonable amount of financial security. They can have that comfortable retirement — but they don't want to relax and chill out. They want more from their 60s, 70s, 80s, and even 90s — and reject the traditional passive life of retirement.

For some, the way forward has been to get involved in voluntary work or with their local communities.

For others, their path has led them to look for ways to boost their retirement income by working — or even to start their own business.

In this chapter, we're talking about your later life career. Just because you're retiring from your current job and lifestyle, doesn't mean you have to retire from action.

Volunteering

In 2016, Saga did some research that found volunteering is extremely popular among the over-50s. A survey of nearly 11,000 people aged 50 or over found 42 percent volunteer for either a charity or local group.

Most said they volunteer to help others, to keep socially active, and for fun.

You have a lifetime's worth of knowledge, skills, and experience you could share with young people, charities, and social groups.

Volunteering is a great way to give back to your community and society at large.

You'll see real benefits to your health by keeping your mind and body active.

There are endless opportunities available suitable for all interests from health and caring to finance and legal. Here are just a few ideas:

- You could do the books for a small local charity.

- Become a mentor for a younger person in your profession.
- Visit local people who are housebound and spend time with them.
- Become a dog walker for an animal charity or shelter.
- Offer to plant gardens for local communities.
- Work in charity shops.
- Drive people to hospital appointments or collect shopping for those who can't get out.
- Help out at your local allotments.

To find the perfect volunteering opportunity near you take a look at Do It at www.do-it.org.

Boosting Your Retirement Income

We've already covered how to maximise your state pension and choose an appropriate private pension in previous chapters.

So what else can you do to generate more income in your retirement?

Well — you don't have to retire completely at all. You can work for longer if you want to, because your employer can no longer insist that you retire when you reach age 65. You may decide to work part-time rather than full-time.

If this isn't possible or you've had enough of your job, you can join a growing number of people who are turning their homes into additional income. You can rent out a room to a lodger. Alternatively you can use websites like Airbnb and HomeAway to rent out some or all of your home for overnight stays.

If you don't like the idea of strangers sleeping in your home, you might want to look at an alternative: rent out part or all of your home for the day. Would your space be suitable for business meetings, club meetings, or even fitness studios? If so, take a look at www.vrumi.com and see what you can offer. It's a great way to get some income for parts of your home you're not using.

If you live in a city, near a train station, near a hospital or airport, or anywhere where parking is in high demand you may want to consider renting out your driveway. This has the potential to bring in income of up to £200 per month — more if you live in a high-demand area like central London.

Visit www.parklet.co.uk/parking-rental-price-guide.aspx has a price guide calculator which calculates how much you could expect to rent out your parking space for per month. We tested it for parking spaces near our Windsor office, and it calculated an income of between £104 and £145 per month.

A space near our Fulham Broadway office in West London would bring in income of £404 to £494 per month — location makes a big difference.

A Google search brings up lots of information on renting out parking spaces. There are websites that offer a "done for you" service where you simply list your property and the times your parking space is available and they do the rest — but they do charge a commission fee when you rent out your space. See www.justpark.com/rent-out-a-parking-space for further information.

They are also many other sites such as Park Let and Park on My Drive and, of course, Gumtree — where you can list just about anything.

It's important to make sure you have a contract with the person renting your space and a number of websites provide this for you. You can find an example of a basic contract at www.parkonmydrive.com/pdf/pomd-contract.pdf.

Just a few things to note — income from your rental space will be taxable as income from land and property. If you don't already receive a tax return contact your tax office to let them know you're receiving income from renting a parking space.

Other things you'll need to check include whether your insurance covers any liability. If you have a mortgage, check whether you need the lender's consent to rent out your parking space. Check planning permission requirements, too. If you rent your property check with your landlord before you rent your space.

Finally, look into the small print to understand what you're committing to and make sure you feel comfortable having someone else using your property — whether it's an overnight stay or parking in your garage or driveway.

Starting Your Own Business

Statistics show the over-50s are the new business start-up generation. According to the Office of National Statistics there were 4.6 million self-employed people in the UK — and the over-50s account for 43 percent of the start-ups.

Some turn to running their own business for extra income to cover the shortfall brought on by retirement… but for others, it's an opportunity to continue working — and not just working for someone else, but doing something they're passionate about for themselves.

If you think the idea of setting up your own business at your age is scary, consider this: research shows businesses set up by the over-50s are much more likely to still be in business after five years than those set up by younger people. So older entrepreneurs have an edge on their younger counterparts. You have years of experience and often a network of contacts to tap into, but even if that's not the case, it's still possible to start a successful business. We'll look at how to do that later in this chapter.

There's also the health aspect to consider. Dame Sally Davis, the UK's chief medical officer, said in her 2015 annual report that people should consider working until their 70s because "good" work is good for our health. It's estimated that a third of workers will be over 50 by 2020.

Do you think you might want to start a business?

Whether you're looking for an extra income to make up any retirement shortfall, or you want to set up a dream business, you'll need to ask yourself: "Can I really make a success of it?"

The only way to answer that is to do a little soul searching and look at the skills and mindset successful business owners have.

It's not unusual to be unsure if you could run a successful business — particularly if you've never run one before. And it's certainly not for everyone. However, there are certain characteristics that will help if you want to run your own business and make it a success. Here are a few:

- Hard work: running your own business, especially in the early days, can be very time consuming. Your days will often drift beyond 9 – 5.
- Focus: set yourself and your business definitive goals and make sure you reach them.
- Opportunistic: look for opportunities in your market and, after due consideration, be willing to act on them.
- Positive: you'll need to be decisive and enthusiastic to succeed.
- Proactive rather than reactive: don't wait for opportunities to come to you, go out looking for them.
- Good leadership skills: you'll need to be able to lead yourself and others — and make the most of yourself, your colleagues, and your situation.
- Accountability: you'll need to hold yourself accountable and review your goals, and look critically at how you've performed.
- Be willing to learn and grow as a business owner and leader: your business can only be as good as you make it. The better-equipped you are to run your business the better your business will do.
- Be willing to delegate: learning the art of delegation will allow you to grow your business.
- Identify your skills and your weaknesses: consider employing someone to cover your weaknesses or subcontract those services to others.
- Good sense of humour: sometimes things go wrong and

you just have to deal with them — seeing everything as a learning opportunity helps.

It's also worth checking your family and loved ones are supportive of your intention to start a business. If they are, they may be willing to get involved and help you set up and run your business, and there will be many areas you can delegate to them. This will be particularly helpful if their strengths are in areas where you're not so strong.

The final and most important consideration is to research your market: who are your potential customers? Who is your competition? This is crucial in deciding whether or not your business has a good chance of success. You'll need to understand your target market and know whether that market is growing or in decline.

Which competitors are currently working in that market? What market share do they hold? What are they selling and what are their prices/fees?

Finally, who are your potential customers? Where are they and what do they want? Remember, people buy what they want rather than what they need.

What Type of Business Could You Run?

What type of structure do you want to use for your business? The most common forms of business are sole trader, partnership, or limited company. There are pros and cons to forming each type of business, and you'll want to consider them carefully.

Sole Trader

There are only a few formalities to doing business as a sole trader, the most important of which is to make sure you begin by notifying HMRC. You must keep business records so you can calculate profits each year and these will form the basis of how you pay your tax and national insurance.

Any profits generated as a sole trader are automatically yours and are taxed accordingly. However, because the business is not separate from your personal affairs, any debts that arise in connection with the business are payable by you.

Partnership

This is an extension of being a sole trader. In a partnership, two or more people will come together to form a business. They pool their talents, clients, and business contacts so that, collectively, they can build a more successful business than they would individually. The partners agree to share the joint profits in pre-determined percentages.

It's an excellent idea to draw up a Partnership Agreement setting the rules of how the partners will work together.

Partners are taxed in the same way as sole traders, but only on their own share of the partnership profits.

As with sole traders, both partners are legally liable to pay the debts of the business. You need to be aware that each partner is "jointly and severally" liable for the partnership debts, so if certain partners are unable to pay their share of the partnership debts, those debts can fall on the other partners.

Limited Company

A limited company is a separate legal entity from its owners. It can trade, own assets, and incur liabilities in its own right. Your ownership of the company is recognised by owning shares in that company. If you also work for the company, you are both the owner (shareholder) and an employee of that company.

When a company generates profits, the profits belong to the company. If you wish to extract money from the company, you must either pay a dividend to the shareholders or a salary as an employee, or both. This is advantageous because you can pay yourself a balance of dividends and salary to minimise your overall tax and national insurance liability.

Companies themselves pay corporation tax on their profits after paying your salary but before distributing your dividends. Effective tax planning means considering profits, salary, and dividends together.

There are extra administrative factors to consider when running a company, including preparing statutory accounts and company secretarial obligations. A big advantage of owning a limited company is your personal liability is limited to the nominal share capital you've invested or any other debts you've personally guaranteed.

It's possible to buy new companies relatively cheaply in a ready-made form usually referred to as "off the shelf" companies.

Is Buying a Franchise an Option For You?

Will you go it alone and start your business from scratch, or could you buy a franchise which provides ready-made systems and processes and intellectual property — effectively a "business in a box", which means you can get up and running quickly.

Franchises are available in all kinds of businesses. Perhaps you'll become a landlord and enter the rental sector with buy-to-let properties, or maybe you'll buy a café franchise and create a caffeinated haven.

Whatever you choose to do, starting a business is a big decision and you must be prepared to put in the time and effort to ensure its success.

What's Stopping You?

Many people are put off starting their own business because they fear it will fail. But the truth is, for every business that fails there's always a good reason and there's always something the business owner could have done differently. That can be an empowering thought for any aspiring business owner.

Running a business is a science with a dash of luck, not solely a matter of luck or a game of chance. To run a successful business you need to understand the rules, do the right things, and avoid making fatal mistakes.

If we take an overview of a successful business you'll find it stands on three pillars of excellence.

The first pillar is the product or service — the business owner has to have a good product or service to offer their customers and there has to be a market for it.

The second pillar is understanding your ideal client or customer and knowing how to communicate with them — that means having one or more effective sales and marketing channels or funnels in place.

The third pillar is understanding your business finances or, as they say, "knowing your numbers". This allows the business owner to plan ahead, to monitor progress month-by-month, to manage risk, and to scale future business development and growth in a planned and controlled way.

These three pillars are the foundation of any successful business. If you fail to focus and understand what is happening to one or more of the pillars, your business has a high chance of failure. If you master each pillar, though, you'll have a business that can provide the financial security you desire — and give you the freedom to live your 60s, 70s, 80s, and beyond on your terms.

So, what is good financial management? Well, perhaps the easiest way to look at this is to understand what constitutes poor financial management, so you can avoid the mistakes so many failing business owners make.

One of the most common mistakes business owners make is to be reactive rather than proactive when planning their business. If we have a clear vision of what we want to achieve in our lives and what we want the business to provide, we can plan what we need to do to achieve our goal and see how we're going to get there. To do that we need a business plan.

Your Business Plan

Running your business without a carefully prepared business plan is like jumping into your car and heading off on a long journey without knowing where you're going — and without bothering to pick up a map or enter the destination into your sat nav system.

A business plan allows you to create and plan what you want your business to achieve for you. It's an opportunity to set out your purpose and vision for the business and clearly set out your goals so you can decide how you're going to reach them.

In short, it's a road map for your business. Your business plan is a live, working document that you'll update as your business grows and review as it reaches each milestone in its journey towards success.

So, with your business plan set out you're ready to move on and think about the numbers in your business — financial management. By financial management I'm not referring to your annual accounts made up by your accountant sometime after your year-end. Annual accounts have their purpose, they won't allow you to look ahead and set the financial goals for your business.

One of the problems with annual accounts is they're retrospective and look back over the last year of trading. They're always at least a year out of date.

What I'm referring to is financial management of the year ahead so you have a clear view of what your business will look like over its first year of trading and beyond. It's about setting targets then monitoring progress through the coming months to make sure you stay on course. If you fall behind you can reset your targets and goals, adjust your anticipated outcomes and look at making some changes within your business. You'll be able to deal with any issues as they arise to prevent them from becoming a serious problem.

If the very thought of dealing with the financial side of your business makes your blood run cold then stay with me, because it's not as horrifying as you may think. Even if you delegate the financial management to someone else, you really need to make sure you understand what it is you're actually delegating!

Five Steps to Success

There are five main steps you need to work through to start a business and put a sound business and financial management plan in place.

Step 1

Bookkeeping is the first step on your journey to becoming good at financial management. Unless you keep good records you won't have a starting point to build your financial management information. There are many good and easy to use computerised bookkeeping systems available to choose from.

Step 2

The next step is the planning stage. This sets out what you want to achieve with your business over the next twelve months. If you need help setting and achieving goals and are prone to going adrift with your plans, Brian P Moran's book *The 12 Week Year* may be a great help to you.

Remember: when making plans for the future you'll need to make certain assumptions and ensure you allow for any unforeseen changes that may arise if those assumptions should prove to be wrong. When you have your written plan you can move on to step 3.

Step 3

This is where you monitor and measure your achievements by preparing monthly management accounts pulling together all the information you need from the previous month.

Firstly, you need to understand your trading performance: your sales, costs of sales, overhead costs, and profit or loss.

Secondly, you need to understand your cash flows and working capital requirements: how much you're owed and when you'll get paid (your debtors), how much you owe and when you have to make payments to your suppliers (your creditors), any loan or finance repayments, and how much you need to draw from the business yourself. And finally, of course, how much money you have in the bank.

At the end of this process you'll be able to see exactly how your profit or loss is showing up in your business and how your cash flow is looking. You'll repeat these steps each month going forward, giving you up-to-date financial information about your business.

Step 4

Next, you'll check whether you're on target to reach your goals as set out in your business plan. You may not be exactly where you predicted in your plan but you now have the information and awareness you need to take some corrective action.

If you are on target — congratulations!

Step 5

The final step is all about looking to the future and updating your forecast based on your most recent results. You'll look at how you think your business will perform in the coming months. To do that, you'll consider the current market, any new information that's come to light, and how your business has performed to date.

You'll also want to take account of any investment requirements the business may have in the near future, and to allow for any potential variations in your assumptions.

If you've been focused and reached your targets, your planned and actual results will show you reaching your goals. If you've not reached your targets but you have all your information in place, you'll find it far easier to establish why and where you went off course.

If you follow these five steps you'll have the best chance of running a successful business. You'll have the information available to plan your growth and to scale your business. You'll understand the difference between profit and cash flow, and understand how to maximise your profit.

Getting funding for your business will be far easier because you'll have all the relevant financial information to hand and you'll be able to reassure any lenders you understand what's going on in your business. Even if you don't feel confident to grow your business yourself, it will be much easier for you to work with a business consultant who understands business growth, development, and funding because you'll have most, if not all, of the key performance indicators they will need to advise you.

Summary

- Think carefully about what you'll do with your retirement — and make concrete plans, not just pipe dreams that might never happen.
- Consider whether or not you'll have enough money to do what you want to do, and if not, how will you make up that shortfall?
- Have you considered volunteering? If so, check out Do It at www.do-it.org.
- Could you run your own business? Consider the type of business you could run, and make sure you follow the five steps to business success we've just covered.

If you decide to start a business, you'll be joining a band of around half-a-million other silver entrepreneurs who have decided to start their own business after retiring from their full-time job.

If that's you, I'd love it if you shared your story with us. Just get in touch by emailing me at laterliving@parfittcresswell.com.

Whatever you choose to do in your retirement and later years — whether it's cruising around the world, volunteering, running your own business, or a mix of them all — we wish you every success for the future.

And remember: your future is in your hands. You have the power to have a wonderful retirement and later life — all it takes is careful planning and expert advice.

In Chapter 13, I'll introduce you to an extraordinary lady who'll share with you the key to successful later living: mindset.

Your Notes

Chapter 13

The Key to Successful Later Living: Mindset

"Your mind is so powerful. Your thoughts will make you or break you, and you are free to think as you want, whenever you want." So says a friend of mine, Vicki La Bouchardiere. She's quite right, too.

How we think and how we choose to act determines the life we lead.

We can choose to be passive, drifting wherever life takes us... or we can choose to take control and build the kind of life we want to live.

That kind of choice isn't just for the young. It's for all of us, no matter what age we are.

You have the power to create a wonderful retirement for yourself and live your life to the full, despite all the challenges and circumstances you may believe are holding you back. You don't need to be rich to have a meaningful, full and interesting life in your later years.

But you also have the power to give away that choice to

governments, to age, to illness, and to infirmity. I hope you choose the former, not the latter.

We are all capable of so much more than we think we are. So I'd like to introduce you to a good friend of mine. She's 88 years old, and she's still living a full and active life. I'd love her to write a book about her life but for now, I've persuaded her to talk to you.

This is Hilary's story

Several years into my retirement, I found myself sitting on the floor in WH Smith one day reading those awful glossy magazines aimed at young women and teenage girls. It was research for a little project I'd been asked to help with.

For some reason, a group of schoolgirls had asked me to help them set up a teenage magazine of their own — I had no experience in this area at all! But I was so impressed by their attitude. They were disillusioned by the outlook of all their school friends, who lived, ate, and dreamed about sleazy teenage magazines that didn't help them prepare for life at all.

The girls had asked, "What can we do? How can we help our classmates feel better about themselves so they don't become obsessed with the messages in the glossy magazines?"

So I said, "I think you'd better start your own magazine!"

I had never read one of those magazines before, so they suggested that I should go along to WH Smith to have a look at them.

That little magazine did very well. They got their school friends interested in culture, fashion, films, books, and positive role models.

I think working with them, learning their language, was one of the things that helped me to stay young.

It's funny, because although I retired at 60 from my career as an occupational therapist, I never did really retire from doing things and learning.

I'd always worked very hard both in England and abroad,

so felt it was perfectly okay to retire at 60. I'm so pleased I did, because I had all that experience behind me, but was still young enough to use that experience in other projects that were important to me.

Like the women's social project in Brixton. I helped to set up the Baytree Centre for Women, which trains and mentors women and families who have had difficult lives. They are mostly refugees, single parents, and immigrants, people who find it difficult to get ahead in the normal manner. Helping to set up Baytree was the first thing I did with my retirement.

But I'm getting ahead of myself.

"Never take no for an answer"

I was very lucky as a child. My family was quite well-off and my father — a very jolly paediatrician always full of optimism — instilled in us from a very early age never to take no for an answer. He encouraged us to stick to what we were doing and to find ways around things if they didn't work out.

I owe a lot to the way he brought us up, never to want to give up.

I also owe a lot to my rather unusual Communist Quaker suffragette headmistress at the boarding school I attended during World War II! She was quite a feminist and thought we should all go to university — something I never did because I studied music instead — but she also instilled in us a strong social conscience and the idea of the equality of people from different countries and cultures. This gave us the desire to travel and much later this dream came true.

One landmark experience for me happened at the end of World War II when German prisoners of war in the UK were waiting to be repatriated back to Germany. At the time the British Government encouraged us to invite German prisoners to our homes and schools. At our school, we gave a concert to German prisoners from the local camp and then lent our instruments for them to play to us. I loaned my violin to one of the young prisoners and to my horror the only music they knew from memory was a Nazi March.

I was chilled to the bone to hear my violin playing a Nazi march. But afterwards on socialising I learnt that he was friendly and kind. I'm from a Jewish family, and my father had brought twelve Jewish children out of Nazi Germany without their parents on the kinder transport. Later these twelve children would become my extended family.

I was in utter confusion. It was a moment that made me think about war and my preconceived ideas about whole nations being "the enemy" or being bad were suddenly challenged. I realised that when you meet and know a person individually from the "enemy" country you think, "This guy can't really help it. It is what he knew, it is what he'd been taught, and his circumstances had forced him into it."

I knew he was from Hamburg and I'd heard his town had been totally flattened. I imagined him going back to his hometown, sitting in the rubble without a home, so I sent him a Red Cross food parcel. Whether it ever reached him I shall never know.

But that experience taught me evil doesn't apply to a whole nation. It applies to a few people, and the rest are good people who are caught up in it.

"Travel as much as possible"

Having started out life as a professional violinist, there came a time when I wanted to change my career to one in which I could help other people. Although I wanted to travel, when I decided to become an occupational therapist I thought I'd have to stay in England for the rest of my life. However, my career as a therapist turned quickly into travel, although all previous attempts to travel had never worked out.

As my father had always taught us, I never gave up — so when I was invited to work in Switzerland to help start up occupational therapy there, I jumped at the opportunity. I worked there for two years, then was invited to go to Argentina to join a team to start a school of occupational therapy in Buenos Aires, where they had a very serious polio epidemic.

I'd recently converted to Catholicism, so I blame God a little bit for all this excitement! I was looking for what He wanted me to do with my life.

During my five years in Argentina, I was very happy to be part of the team that helped to introduce the occupational therapy discipline to the country.

After the people finished their rehabilitation in the centre I used to visit them in their homes to see how they were getting on. Often I would find young paralysed men sitting in their wheelchairs with nothing to do, very often unable to go out.

The rehabilitation centre where we worked had a wonderful sports complex. One of the men I visited had been in the Paralympic basketball team, but was unable to do anything in his home. So that gave me an idea to tackle this need — I decided to change the direction of my work and to specialise in employment rehabilitation, so people could get into jobs they could do, which was unheard of in Argentina back then.

From there, I was invited to go to Chile to do the same. For the last ten years of my career in South America, I worked with the ILO (International Labor Organization) to set up training and assessment for disabled people, helping them to get into work.

I've always focused on what people can do, not on what they can't do.

I think that is the key to living a full, happy life, whatever age you are — especially in old age.

"Staying sociable and making connections is so important"

I find, the older I get, it's not always easy to get out and stay active. But I find I feel best when I'm with other people of all ages, becoming part of their lives rather than dwelling on my own limitations.

Last Sunday, for example, I thought I didn't have the energy to go out to be with close friends of mine — but I made myself go, and I'm so pleased that I did. I had a wonderful time and met some new people.

Staying sociable and making connections is so important. You must notice, when you pass people in the street they often seem very stressed! You see they're worried, and you think there must be so many problems in that person's life. Yet when you smile, you get a smile back and make a connection.

Making that connection with people and taking the time to be aware of them is so important. It's easy not to see the person behind the till or behind the counter. Talk to them. Most people love to talk and that can really help ease loneliness, especially if you live alone.

I know it's more difficult for housebound people, but I'm sure everyone can make the most of the opportunity of a delivery service — such as supermarket deliveries, or the postman.

Thinking too much about how you feel, if you're tired or low on energy, can stop you from living a full life. It's too easy to look inwards and focus on yourself when you're having a bad day, and let that stop you from getting on and living life.

"I focus on the things I can do, rather than the things I can't do"

I focus on the things I can do, rather than the things I can't do. It probably comes from my profession! In rehabilitation and occupational therapy, you focus on your patient's skills, not their limitations. You try to help them find their skills and channel their energy into them. We can all do that, I think.

But as I said before, I find as time goes on, I have less energy. I used to be out and about a lot, visiting people, going to the shops, museums, exhibitions, but now I don't have the energy to do all that. I don't go on the Tube anymore because stairs are difficult. I'm lucky to have a good bus service, which makes a difference.

So I try to make the effort to do things when I don't feel like it. It's rather like when you smile, it makes you feel happier. I practice smiling in the mirror! Start your day off with a smile. See how much prettier you look! Smiling helps you feel more optimistic, too.

We can all do so much more than we think and can all learn something new every day.

So for me, new experiences are something to be treasured. Life never ends in this sense, because it's all new experiences. I rather like change, and I always enjoy learning something new, which turns simple, sometimes insignificant things into great pleasures.

I can give you a small example from my life recently. I had to return an article to Amazon, which was a totally new experience for me. I was sweating away on the computer trying to work out how to do it, and someone came and gave me a hand in the end. Then I had to find a special place to take the parcel to — it was this little shop I'd passed many times but had no idea what they did! It was such a joy to find this new facility nearby.

"I don't think about getting older"

I try to say I'm growing younger every day, even though I do have to catch myself many times from moaning about my limitations. That helps me to be grateful instead, because so many other people are in such terrible situations.

For me to go down the road to the corner shop to get a paper is as much as I can do some days. On other days, I can do more. I feel that's great. It's enough. As long as I go out and do what I can.

I don't think about getting older, instead, I think about seeing my friends and family and having a good time with them and finding out about their lives.

Getting older really is all about adapting to life as you change and as it changes around you. I was never much of a reader because I was always out doing things — but now I'm enjoying reading and watching TV programmes I didn't watch before. Recently I followed the Olympics when they were on. So there is a plus to being less active.

"What does the future hold?"

I do sometimes wonder about the future. After all, I'm going to get worse, not better as I get older. I'm curious about how long I'm going to live, and how I'm going to die. Everyone wonders about this I'm sure.

But one can't solve anything by thinking about it. In the end, you get the most you can out of each day and enjoy life by living each moment to the full.

My main advice then is not to think about oneself too much, which can be very hard when living on one's own. There is always something interesting to do to fill your days with.

I'm very thankful to God I've still got all my marbles — so my biggest frustration is my body not being able to keep up with my mind! It's a gradual decline, though, so I'm always very pleased I'm able to do the things I can do.

I was very pleased recently when I was asked to participate in a workshop when I thought I was past my sell-by date! But it turned out that I could still truly contribute. Interest in people and helping them seems to be key for staying young and active.

"Find help where you can"

If one can, it is important to keep up with the younger generation. As we get older we have so much welcome experience we can share with them. They also need someone to listen to them, in whom they can confide. At the same time it keeps us in touch with what is happening around us.

In my case I am fortunate to live in a house surrounded by people of all ages doing different kinds of work. And I haven't even mentioned the joy of keeping in touch with one's family.

But I realise that not everyone is fortunate enough to be close to their family and friends. To grow old alone without this kind of network can't be easy.

But I've discovered there is so much going on in the community for older people, which we had no idea existed — or how to connect to it. This can be the answer to our loneliness.

Quite by chance I found out through the Citizen's Advice Bureau about a group in the Borough that provides numerous activities for people over 50: computer classes for beginners, salsa dancing classes, and pilates — which I do when I can, once a week. There are also reading groups, regular cultural outings, and more. They offer exercises for people in wheelchairs and balance programmes to help reduce the risk of falling. And of course you meet other people, and that's very good.

Some councils are better than others at providing you with information about what's going on, and the different kind of services you can get. However, if you look for it, once you connect with an organisation like the Citizen's Advice Bureau, GPs, social services, or even the local library, you quickly find out about all the available resources.

Summary

I hope you've found Hilary's story inspiring. I think she's an extraordinary woman and is living proof you can live a full, happy life, whatever age you are.

I believe the key is to focus on what you can do, not what you can't — and ask for help and advice if you need it.

You are capable of so much more than you think you are — we all are.

And I'm hoping this book has given you a good place to start planning for your future.

In the final chapter, you'll find a later living checklist so you can make sure you've got everything covered.

Your Notes

The Later Living Checklist

Planning for your later years isn't about being morbid. In fact, I believe this type of planning is just the opposite of having a bleak outlook on life and death.

Proper planning doesn't just enable you to live a life of fun, ease, and comfort in your later years, it also lessens the impact of death when it happens (hopefully later rather than sooner).

Grief is difficult enough to cope with on its own. The last thing anyone wants is to have to wade through a minefield of financial woes, too. So planning early and planning well is a great idea. Your later years can be fun, fulfilling, and well-planned — which is what this book is all about.

Talk things through with your family sooner rather than later. Burying your head in the sand only stores up trouble. Instead of having an "unpleasant conversation", why not turn the occasion into a positive and empowering event? Tell your spouse, your children, or your parents what your plans are. Explain the type of life you want to live, and what you may be worried about. Reminisce about the past and plan for the future.

Use this book as a guide.

Everything you need to know about later life finances, wills, housing and care homes, along with practical considerations, is in here. And to tie it all up, this last section contains a handy checklist so you know you've got everything covered.

- Sort out your will. If you do nothing else, do this one thing.
- Decide who's going to look after your children, or anyone who depends on you, after you're gone.
- Make sure your pets will be looked after.
- If your estate is likely to be worth more than £325,000 get proper advice on inheritance tax planning (and do it as soon as possible so your beneficiaries get everything you want them to get).
- Put a power of attorney in place while you're still fully able to do so — who would look after your financial affairs and make decisions for you if you lost your mental faculties?
- Put together a financial fact sheet with all the details of your bank accounts, pension, utility bills, and anything else people will need to know once you're gone (but don't list your passwords with them!).
- Make sure your partner, children, parents, or other trusted person has the practical skills they need to look after the family finances if something should happen to you.
- Plan your funeral so your loved ones don't have to make difficult decisions when they're grieving.
- Consider taking out a funeral plan to cover the costs of your funeral, so you and your family don't have to worry about it.
- If you're younger with younger children, consider taking out life insurance so your family will be looked after if anything happens to you.
- Get professional advice from a later life financial adviser so you can make the most of your cash and assets — and

remember, you can't take it with you so don't suffer in life to save for when you're gone!

- Think about the kind of home you want to live in as you get older and the type of care you might need.
- Consider getting professional help for downsizing, choosing care homes if relevant, making a will or an LPA, and planning your finances.

Remember, many professionals will offer you a free consultation to talk through what you need. Take them up on it, because even if you decide to go it alone, that consultation will give you all kinds of valuable information. In the *Further Information* section, you'll find contact details for my law firm, as well as contact details for the professionals who've contributed to this book.

Once you've planned all the important things, get busy living! Take that holiday you've always wanted to have. See the sights you've always wanted to see. With proper planning and advice, you can probably afford to live much more fully than you might think.

Your Notes

Further Information

Legal Information

Parfitt Cresswell Windsor Office
17-21 Victoria Street, Windsor, Berkshire, SL4 1HE.
Telephone: 01753 271640
Fax: 01753 850776
Email: windsor@parfittcresswell.com

Parfitt Cresswell Central London Office
53-59 Chandos Place, London, WC2N 4HS.
Telephone: 0207 078 0846
Fax: 0207 381 4044
Email: enquiries@parfittcresswell.com

Parfitt Cresswell West London Office
593-599 Fulham Road, London, SW6 5UA.
Telephone: 0207 381 8311
Fax: 0207 381 4044
Email: enquiries@parfittcresswell.com

Parfitt Cresswell Reading Office
2a-2b Prospect Street, Caversham, Reading, Berkshire, RG4 8JG
Telephone: 01184 020881
Fax: 01189 474410
Email: reading@parfittcresswell.com

Parfitt Cresswell Haywards Heath Office
Colemans, Paddockhall Chambers, Paddockhall Road, Haywards Heath, West Sussex RH16 1HF
Telephone: 01444 459555
Fax: 01444 440306
Email: law@colemans-solicitors.com

Parfitt Cresswell Tunbridge Wells Office
Keene Marsland, 6 Clanricarde Gardens, Tunbridge Wells, Kent, TN1 1PH
Telephone: 01892 526442
Fax: 01892 510486
Email: enquiries@keenemarsland.co.uk

Parfitt Cresswell Tunbridge Wells Office
Max Barford & Co, 6 Clanricarde Gardens, Tunbridge Wells, Kent ,TN1 1PH
Telephone: 01892 539379
Fax: 01892 521874
Email: enquiries@maxbarford.co.uk

Parfitt Cresswell Edenbridge Office
Jevons Riley & Pope, 2c High Street, Edenbridge, Kent, TN8 5AG
or 11 High Street, Edenbridge, Kent, TN8 5AB
Telephone: 01732 864411
Fax: 01732 866921
Email: admin@jrplaw.co.uk

Pensions Information
David Allan, APFS and Stephen Wilson, BA (Hons) DipPFS
2h Wealthcare LLP
22 Wycombe End
Beaconsfield
Buckinghamshire
HP9 1NB
Tel: 01494 683100
Fax: 01494 683101
Email: david.allan@2hwealthcare.co.uk
www.2hwealthcare.co.uk

Care Home Information
Debbie Harris
Chosen With Care
Telephone: 01892 300530
Email: debbie@chosenwithcare.co.uk
www.chosenwithcare.co.uk

Downsizing Information
Felicity Bunt
Senior Services
Telephone: 07939 042 805
Email: felicity@seniorservicesmanagment.co.uk
www.seniorservicesmanagement.co.uk

You can also find a wealth of information on Age UK's website:
www.ageuk.org.uk

Thank You

An Invitation

As a thank you for reading *The Later Living Guide*, I'd like to invite you to apply for a free initial consultation at one of our offices.

If you're ready to talk to a lawyer and want to plan your future, I'd like to invite you to apply for a free, face-to-face initial meeting (valued at £200) with one of our expert private client lawyers. Our team can help you with will writing and estate planning, lasting powers of attorney, deputyships, trusts, probate, and estate administration.

You can come to any of our offices and make sure you find a lawyer who understands your individual needs and will look after your best interests.

Your retirement and future comfort are in your hands. You can react to what happens to you and leave it up to chance... or you can choose to be proactive and create the kind of lifestyle you dream of for your later years.

Simply call us on 0800 999 4437 or email laterliving@parfittcresswell.com and book a time to come and tell us about your future plans.

About the Author

I'm Teresa Payne, owner at Parfitt Cresswell. Growing up I never dreamt of being a lawyer... Until I found myself facing divorce in my late 20s. I had a seven-year-old son and the last thing I thought I'd experience was my relationship ending and having to start again.

To be honest, I didn't know where to turn. The road ahead felt like an enormous mountain and I didn't have the emotional or physical strength to even take the first step of the climb. Fortunately, I had a good friend who supported me through this. With her encouragement, I went along to my local solicitors feeling confident they'd be able to help me.

They were qualified professionals and advertised "family law" so I thought I was in good hands. I think most would agree that was a reasonable assumption — but after experiencing their non-existent client care and paying substantial legal fees for a very poor service and very little practical advice, I decided I could do far better than this myself.

I started researching "how to divorce", "what happens to the family home when couples separate", and "where will the children live after divorce" — all those questions that wake you up in the night when it feels like your world is falling apart.

My Mission In Life

My research was daunting and time-consuming but it sparked an interest to learn more about our legal system. This interest, and my desire to help others going through the legal maze, changed my direction in life. I decided to use the funds I received from my divorce to train as a solicitor — and spent the next seven years studying until I qualified in 2004.

At the start of my professional life I worked face-to-face, individually, with many clients helping them through some of the most difficult times in their lives. And I helped people plan for the end of their lives, too. It was so rewarding to help others navigate the legal and emotional maze and help people realise their later years can be fun, fulfilling, and exciting.

As my client numbers grew I realised I needed more "me's" if I was going to fulfil my mission of helping as many people as possible navigate the often difficult-to-understand legal process. So in 2007 I bought my own law firm, Parfitt Cresswell. We started in a small office in Fulham Broadway in West London.

Over the past ten years, I've focused on growing specialist expert teams in three key areas that impact most of us at some point during our lives. Those three areas are Private Client, Family Law, and Property Law.

Our private client area covers will writing and estate planning, lasting powers of attorney, deputyships, trusts, probate, and estate administration. This book covers these areas in detail.

We also have a specialist family law team and a property law team. Our expert teams of qualified lawyers all share the same values as I do. They work hard to provide the very best standards of client support and legal advice to all our clients.

They're all experts in their own specialist area and know exactly how to advise you for your particular situation.

My team also understands the emotional pressures you may be going through and will support you and, in some cases, introduce you to other professionals who can help — like financial planners and care home advisors.

My mission is very clear — I want to help you get the most out of your later years. I want you to have peace of mind and choice, so you don't have to make decisions in crisis. And I want you to be able to leave your children and dependents with a well-managed situation and perhaps a nest egg of their own.

We're not here to push you into making one-size-fits-all decisions. We're here to help you make the best decisions possible for you and your family.

We're here to help people who are looking for expert help navigating through the later years of life. People who want to achieve the best lifestyle they can in their circumstances — and leave behind something for their family's future. Because of this, we ask all our clients to meet us in person for a free consultation. This gives you the opportunity to tell us about your situation and your goals, and it gives us the opportunity to show you what we offer. We only accept clients we believe we can work with and truly help.

Give us a call on: 0800 999 4437.

Or email: laterliving@parfittcresswell.com

And book your meeting today.

Whichever route you choose I and my team wish you well in your future.

Teresa J Payne
Parfitt Cresswell

Glossary

Ageing in Place: older people living in the residence of their choice for as long as they are able, often with support services.

Annuity: a type of insurance policy or investment that provides a regular income, usually in exchange for an upfront lump sum investment. When used for long-term care, they provide a guaranteed income for life to help pay for care costs.

Assets: an item of value owned by a person or company, regarded as having value and available to meet debts, commitments, or legacies.

Assisted living: a system of housing and limited care that is designed for people who need some help with daily activities but don't need care in a nursing home.

Attorney: a person authorised to act and make decisions on another's behalf.

Bankruptcy: a legal proceeding involving a person or business that is unable to repay outstanding debts.

Beneficiary: a person designated as the recipient of funds or other property under a will or trust.

Bequeath: leave something (e.g. property) to a person or other beneficiary by a will.

Capital Gains Tax: a tax levied on profit from the gift, transfer, or sale of property or an investment.

Care home: a generic term for residential and nursing homes.

Care Quality Commission (CQC): the independent regulator of all health and social care services in England.

Court of Protection: a superior court of record created under the Mental Capacity Act 2005. It has jurisdiction over the property, financial affairs and personal welfare of people who lack mental capacity to make decisions for themselves.

Dementia care home: can be either residential or nursing homes but they also cater for residents who have dementia.

Deprivation of assets: intentionally reducing assets — such as money, property or income — so these won't be included in the financial assessment for paying care home fees.

Donor: a person who makes a Power of Attorney document giving authority to another person to make decisions for them.

Enduring Power of Attorney: a document made before October 1, 2007, to appoint attorneys to make financial and property decisions on your behalf.

Estate: all the money and items of value (e.g. personal belongings, shares, investments, or property) owned by a particular person.

Executor: a person or institution appointed by a testator to carry out the terms of their will.

Fiduciary duty: the highest standard of care.

HMRC: Her Majesty's Revenue and Customs is a non-ministerial department of the UK Government responsible for the collection of taxes.

Income tax: tax levied directly on personal income.

Inheritance tax (IHT): tax charged on assets as the result of a person dying, or on assets passing into trusts.

Intestate: a person who has died without having made a will.

Lasting Power of Attorney (LPA): a legal document that lets you (the donor) appoint one or more people (attorneys) to help you make financial and property or health and welfare decisions or to make those types of decisions on your behalf if you lose mental capacity.

Living will: a written statement detailing a person's desires regarding future medical treatment in circumstances in which they are no longer able to express informed consent, especially regarding life-sustaining treatment.

Mental capacity: being able to make your own decisions.

Nursing home: a residential care home with extra nursing care — registered nurses are on-site 24/7.

Office of the Public Guardian: a government body that, under the Mental Capacity Act 2005, protects the private assets and supervises the financial affairs of people who lack mental capacity for making decisions. It keeps record of all registered EPAs and LPAs.

Ordinary Power of Attorney: allows one person (or more), known as your attorney(s), to make financial decisions on your behalf. It is only valid while you still have mental capacity to make your own decisions.

Personal care: support with washing, dressing, eating, toileting.

Power of Attorney: the authority to act for another person in specified or all legal or financial matters.

Probate: the official legal proving of a will. A legal process following which the court produces a document called the Grant of Probate confirming the executor's authority to deal with the estate of the person who has died.

Remaindermen: a person (or persons) entitled to receive a remainder interest in any asset — usually the ultimate beneficiaries of a will.

Residential care: long-term care given to people who stay in a residential setting rather than in their own home or family home.

Respite care: a temporary stay in a care home by a person to provide respite for their regular carers.

Senior Move Management: the profession that helps older people and their families with the practical, physical, and emotional aspects of moving home or "Ageing in Place".

Testator: a person who has made a will.

Trust: an arrangement whereby a person (a trustee) holds assets as its nominal owner for the good of one or more beneficiaries.

Trustees: people who run the trust during the trust's lifetime. In a will trust, this is usually the executors, but you can appoint separate trustees.

Will: a legal document in which a person specifies the method to be applied in the management and the distribution pattern of their estate after their death.

Index

B

C

H

I

M